Praise for *Four Levers Negotiating*

"I have worked with hundreds and hundreds of sellers over my career, and without question, Todd's *Four Levers Negotiating* is the most clear, actionable, and effective tool I have ever brought into a selling organization. Ever. Hands down. No question. It works because it's honest, true, and seeks to arrive at an outcome that is mutually beneficial."

—Ethan Zoubek, President, Atari

"I have always believed in building trust and embracing transparency in selling, and Todd Caponi articulates these principles better than anyone I've encountered. In *Four Levers Negotiating*, he delivers an innovative, actionable methodology that is both practical and grounded in the realities of today's buyer. His approach has become the foundation for how my team not only negotiates but also communicates with prospects and customers—with honesty, clarity, and impact for all."

—Ken Hohenstein, Chief Revenue Officer, OneStream Software

"*Four Levers Negotiating* connects the dots between how we sell and how we negotiate. Todd Caponi shows us that trust doesn't end with the yes—it begins there."

—David Woodbury, Chief Commercial Officer, Sodexo

"*Four Levers Negotiating* is the antidote to the outdated, manipulative tactics that plague sales negotiations. Todd Caponi offers a simple, human-centered approach that builds trust, not tension, and leads with transparency. Required reading for any sales professional, regardless of tenure."

—Samantha McKenna, Founder, #samsales Consulting

"I wish I had this book earlier in my career. Todd's Four Levers make every sales negotiation feel less like a battle and more like a collaboration. You'll close better deals, build better relationships, and sleep better at night."

—David (DP) Pietrese, Chief Revenue Officer, Recorded Future

"*Four Levers Negotiating* is like replacing your hostage negotiation manual with a human one. It strips out the hostage-theatrics and hands you a framework built for today's messy, transparent, post-trust market where buyers talk, pricing leaks, and trust wins. Todd's last two books were required reading, and this one is no different. Or you can just keep offering 'one-time discounts' that mysteriously reappear every quarter."

—Matt Green, Chief Revenue Officer, Sales Assembly

"This is the book on negotiation that your buyers want you to read. Todd brings such a refreshing, actionable point of view to one of the trickiest sales skills: negotiation. If you want to protect your margin, without losing your buyer's trust, read this today."

—Jen Allen-Knuth, Founder, DemandJen

"*Four Levers Negotiating* is the rare sales book that actually makes your job easier. Todd gives sellers a smarter, more honest way to approach pricing and negotiation—one that builds trust and drives better results."

—Jeff Rosset, Chief Executive Officer, Sales Assembly

"*Four Levers Negotiating* is a terrific foundation for sales negotiation and creates a clear, grounding framework for reps to be effective, consistent, and clear about how a customer can impact their cost of goods or service purchased. It also creates a shared language for sales reps and leaders and leads to a short hand of deal maturity and likelihood of close! Don't sleep on this one."

—Richard Ortega, Chief Revenue Officer, accessiBe

FOUR
LEVERS
Negotiating

ALSO BY TODD CAPONI

The Transparency Sale

The Transparent Sales Leader

FOUR LEVERS
Negotiating

THE SIMPLE, COUNTERINTUITIVE WAY TO HIGHER DEAL VALUES AND LASTING TRUST

TODD CAPONI

MATT HOLT

Matt Holt Books
An Imprint of BenBella Books, Inc.
Dallas, TX

Four Levers Negotiating copyright © 2026 by Todd Caponi

MATT HOLT BenBella

Matt Holt is an imprint of BenBella Books, Inc.
8080 N. Central Expressway
Suite 1700
Dallas, TX 75206
benbellabooks.com
Send feedback to feedback@benbellabooks.com

BenBella and *Matt Holt* are federally registered trademarks.

Printed in the United States of America
10 9 8 7 6 5 4 3 2 1

Library of Congress Control Number: 2025033538
ISBN 9781637748404 (hardcover)
ISBN 9781637748411 (electronic)

Editing by Joe Rhatigan
Copyediting by Michael Fedison
Proofreading by Lisa Story and Jenny Bridges
Text design and composition by PerfecType, Nashville, TN
Cover design by Tom McKeveny
Printed by Lake Book Manufacturing

Special discounts for bulk sales are available. Please contact bulkorders@benbellabooks.com.

To my wife, Christy

Contents

The knowledge of buyers has increased, and they are no longer disposed to pay what is asked of them, unless persuaded in their minds that the sellers regulate their prices on some sound basis.

—Thomas Herbert Russell,
Salesmanship: Theory and Practice, 1910

Introduction

> In a skillfully finished sale, there should be neither
> victor nor vanquished. The selling process is not
> a battle of minds. There is no room in it for any
> spirit of antagonism on the part of the salesman.
> —*Norval A. Hawkins*, Certain Success, 1920

Growing up, my hobby was collecting baseball cards. The local 7-Eleven convenience store was less than a mile from my childhood home, a quick bike ride with my friends. Whenever we mustered up even a dollar, we were off to buy a pack or two. Back then, a pack of baseball cards cost around 35 cents each, containing 15 cards plus a hard stick of powdery gum with enough flavor to last an entire minute or two.

Then the real fun began. We would rip open the packs, chomp our gum sticks, and begin negotiations.

"I'll give you this Nolan Ryan for your Pete Rose."

"What? Are you crazy? Pete Rose has more hits than any player in history."

"But Nolan Ryan is the all-time strikeouts leader. His card is totally worth more than yours, and I need that one to complete my Phillies collection."

The "horse trading" was fun. Each card had a different value, based solely on what we, as individual children, believed the value was of what we had to offer versus our perceived value of what we were trying to acquire. Establishing values based on random feelings, justified by cherry-picked logic regarding the performance and careers of the individual players, worked. Following a transaction, it wouldn't take long for us to determine who won or lost the negotiation. The winner was sure to let the loser know. The loser was none too ready to accept defeat.

Fast-forward 15 years or so. I'm a salesperson. It didn't take too long for me to realize there was something wrong with the way we were expected to negotiate transactions with our customers.

Considering the responsibilities of a sales professional, doesn't it seem strange that the personality that is required to make the sale has to change completely when it comes time to negotiate the transaction? The greatest selling professionals wholeheartedly focus on helping their customers achieve optimal outcomes. They serve their clients and take on the role of a navigator and guide, playing the long game through strong relationships.

However, once the client says yes, we tend to shift personalities. Now our focus turns to our own outcomes, not the customer's. According to Jeffrey Rubin in his 1983 article "Negotiation" in *American Behavioral Scientist*, "Typically, each side begins by asking for more than it expects to get, and through a series of offers and counteroffers in a stepwise concession process, a mutually acceptable agreement is ultimately reached."[1]

In other words, at the most important point of the selling process, we intentionally start lying.

The craziest part, to me, is how salespeople learn and execute traditional negotiation strategies. Worst case, the negotiation strategies taught in most sales organizations are simply advanced versions of my childhood experiences with baseball cards. Best case, we learn techniques from former high-stakes negotiators from the FBI and CIA used to release hostages from bank heists, appease warring nations, and settle economic disruptions caused by massive union labor disagreements.

As a salesperson, I hated negotiating sales transactions. It felt gross. I wanted to maintain my relationships with my clients, not erode them at the most important point in the journey—right at the goal line. If I could avoid negotiating on behalf of my organization, all the better.

Salespeople sell stuff—products and services. We are not negotiating union labor contracts or peace treaties between warring countries, and if we don't win the negotiation, people don't die. We don't get to tase the individual we are negotiating with and drag them to jail afterward.

If we are to believe that authenticity, transparency, and trust are the three cores of being a successful salesperson, why wouldn't that extend through the negotiation? To succeed, we must maintain a relationship with this customer—earning their commitment in a way that results in them staying with us, growing with us, advocating for us, and taking us with them to their next job or position.

THE REVELATION

On a hot summer day in Houston, my desire to avoid common negotiation practices met with a high-pressure, multimillion-dollar sale conversation. The result? The easiest and most successful sales negotiation I had ever participated in—and a revelation that turned into a simple structure and approach to negotiations that would serve me and my teams very well over the coming years and eventually end up in the pages of this book.

I had just arrived at the airport—young and brand-new—wearing the traditional Senior Vice President of Sales attire: slacks, a collared shirt, and a sports coat.

My regional sales representative, David, picked me up in his rental car, and we were off to see his largest prospect, a massive oil services company.

David was working on a multiyear, multimillion-dollar opportunity with this account, and they were ready to purchase our 3D product visualization software, designed to assist in building interactive education and marketing assets. We were in the final throes of negotiations, and the client's assigned procurement representative was frustrated. He communicated to David the need to complete the transaction details to begin the implementation. He added, "Every time I have a question regarding the terms, it feels like you have to call your manager for the answer. This is taking way too much time. Instead of speaking to you, the messenger, can we please get your manager in a room so we can finish this?"

Since, indeed, David wasn't empowered to negotiate on our company's behalf, I went to Houston.

Pulling into the parking lot, my expectation was that we would just be meeting with Fred, the procurement representative. (His name wasn't really Fred . . . I just like that name.) We checked in at the front desk, and Fred met us in the lobby and escorted us to a fifth-floor conference room.

The doors opened, and five additional procurement team members from this massive company were waiting for me, prepared to kick my butt. I distinctly remember the look on one woman's face. She looked like a mixed martial arts fighter, markedly excited to beat on a less prepared opponent.

My sports coat felt a little warmer and tighter as my brain began to spin with anxiety. I wasn't prepared for a battle. My level of competency in the negotiation would likely result in a terrible outcome.

It was at this moment that negotiating changed for me.

A week earlier, at our headquarters in Pleasanton, California, I sat along with our chief executive officer (CEO) in the office of our chief financial officer (CFO). The CEO wrote four things on a whiteboard: four key elements that drove the metrics of the organization, or really, every for-profit company in the world.

Back in Houston, maybe to buy myself some time, or maybe just to sound a little smarter, I asked the meeting participants if I could share these four elements on the whiteboard behind them. They obliged.

As it turned out, these four elements became the backbone of the entire negotiation. Trust was built, not eroded. The client paid for every concession we provided in the form of one of the four elements on the board. We left the room as friends, with the terms of a commercial agreement worked out in less than 30 minutes. And when this client desired to purchase our technology for another division of their organization, they used these four elements to negotiate their own terms.

The Four Levers of Negotiation was born.

WHY NOW?

While many believe the sales profession has shifted entirely over the past few years, as a nerd for the history of sales, I don't believe that to be true. However, I do believe two core shifts are fundamental to how we should be thinking about our actions going forward.

1) The "As a Service" Economy

Traditional negotiation approaches were designed during a time when "the deal" was the peak of the sales process. The original approach of what might be considered modern sales was designed during the progressive era of the Industrial Revolution in the early 1900s. Items were being manufactured. Salespeople sold them. The manufactured item was delivered, and that was it. Once the agreement was signed, the sale was complete. The negotiation was a one-time event that happened at the end of the sales cycle.

Today, the sale is no longer the peak of the selling relationship. The sale is simply an early milestone on the path to having a customer who not only buys from you, but stays, buys more, brings you with them to their next role or company, and advocates for you to their friends and peers.

2) The "Feedback" Economy

Traditional negotiation techniques were designed during a time when the consequences of a dissatisfied customer were not what they are today. Even during the last half of the 1900s, if you were oversold, the product didn't do what you thought, or the product just sucked, what were you gonna do, write a letter? Call an 800 number? Tell a couple of buddies at the local watering hole?

Today, the proliferation of feedback, peer connection, and information sharing means the truth will always prevail. Your buyers talk to their peers. They're members of communities. Conversations abound that sound like, *"Hey, did you buy that XYZ product from Acme? Yeah? What did you pay for it?"* Your buyers change jobs. Artificial intelligence will and already is exposing pricing models.

An environment where each customer of yours is paying a different amount based primarily on how well or poorly the negotiation went is no longer sustainable.

Negotiating the terms of an agreement requires consistency. Your pricing structures must be consistent, easily understood, communicated, and . . . transparent.

WHAT THIS BOOK IS . . .

Focused primarily on business-to-business transactions, *Four Levers Negotiating* is designed to be a simple, structured approach to help you confidently deliver, propose, and negotiate using a cards-faceup approach. For the biggest of the big deals to the smallest of the small, by just reading the first few chapters, you will find immediate applications to help your deals become more valuable, and the long-term value of those deals will rise.

You'll share the levers with everyone—you don't have to wait until you've built enough "value" or are speaking to the "right person." You will build trust to and through the goal line of your transactions. Your deals will become more predictable too. As your customers move on to other organizations, they will take you and your solutions with them, and the value of those transactions will rise as well.

WHAT THIS BOOK IS NOT . . .

While there are many lessons throughout the book that can be applied to many other negotiating circumstances, *Four Levers Negotiating* does not apply cleanly to business-to-consumer selling. If you are a real estate agent selling a home, a car salesperson selling a cool new hybrid, or even someone negotiating the sale of your old record collection at a garage sale, you will find the principles make sense but are likely less applicable to those environments. We won't be learning negotiation styles. You won't learn how to maximize your share in a divorce negotiation, slay a union uprising in a labor dispute, or settle land disputes of warring nations.

Negotiating can feel good. Negotiating can be easy. No need to prepare for battle.

CHAPTER 1

The Framework

Consider the other person in negotiations—adapt
your approach and treatment to him personally, his
needs, his circumstances, and his ambitions; and
never let him feel that he is being coerced or rushed.
—Francis Bacon, "Of Negotiating"
(Essay XLVII), 1625

I said, "Before we start, do you mind if I use the whiteboard behind you?
There are four primary levers that drive our pricing model, and really
our entire organization. I thought they might serve as a good guide for
the conversation we're obviously about to have."

They looked at me, uninspired, and replied affirmatively. "Sure, have
fun." (Okay, I don't think they said that, but I could sense the disinterest
in what I was about to write.)

I awkwardly walked around the conference room table, grabbed a dry-erase marker, and started to write.

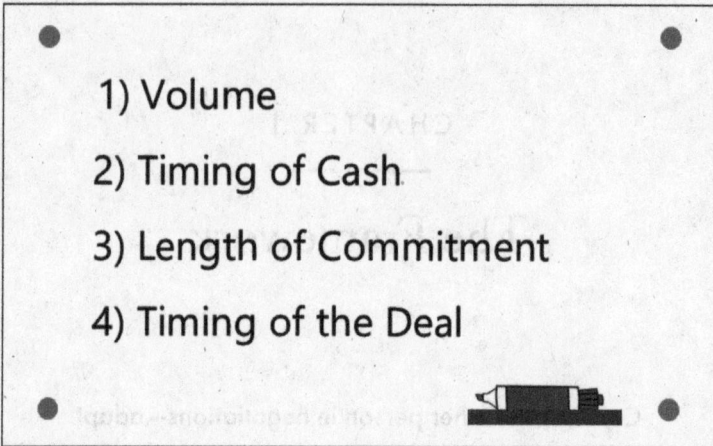

1) Volume

2) Timing of Cash

3) Length of Commitment

4) Timing of the Deal

The six procurement team members looked up at the whiteboard, seemingly unsure what to do with what I had just written. Honestly, I was also unsure what I wanted them to do with what I had written. I guess I had hoped at least one of them would have been impressed by my skillful whiteboard penmanship.

Fred, moving on from what I had just written, officially started the meeting.

"As you are aware, we have been working diligently on finalizing this transaction so this division can get started. We asked you, Todd, to come here so we can speed up the process, eliminate the back-and-forth, and determine whether we will be able to move forward or not. Given where the pricing and terms are on this transaction, due to budget issues, the only way we will be able to move forward is with a reduction in this price of 35%."

Goliath was asking for, almost demanding, a 35% discount! While we knew a discount request would be coming, this was a significant one, at that. This 35% of $2.5 million was $875,000 . . . per year on a proposed three-year commitment. And here we were, one of us named David, having to now defend our price and defeat the giant.

How would you respond? Given my sales upbringing, there are usually two primary ways.

OLD-SCHOOL WAY #1: MAKE THE VALUE OR ROI PITCH

In 1927, Herbert N. Casson wrote in his book *Tips for Traveling Salesmen*,[2] "Never mention price until the customer thinks it is more." It's an approach built upon a perception that the customer will pay any amount if they believe the value, or ROI (return on investment), warrants the higher price.

The truth is, if the customer is asking for a significant discount at the end of the sales cycle, your opportunity to prop up the *value* of your solution has already passed. In this room filled with procurement professionals, their purpose is not to be sold on the value. Their purpose is to finalize an agreement for the most favorable terms possible. In other words, this room full of procurement professionals could not give a single crap about our value. An individual holding a group of hostages is interested only in a helicopter to take them and their bag of loot away to paradise. Nothing else will do.

OLD-SCHOOL WAY #2: FREE DISCOUNTS FOR EVERYONE! (OR, THE PING-PONG APPROACH)

A significant number of organizations I work with today have provided their salespeople with what they believe is a gift to help get deals done.

"Well, 35% is an awful lot. I don't think we can do that. However, I can give you 10% off right now. I don't even have to ask anyone for permission."

Ugh. You've just offered to provide a payment to this multibillion-dollar organization in the form of charity to their bottom line.

And you've just opened the floodgates. You've confirmed that your price isn't really your price. You haven't sped up the journey to a positive conclusion; you have slowed it down.

"Ten percent will not be enough. You will need to do more than that."

The ping-pong match has begun. They admit that 35% off is not their firm desired ending. We come closer. They come closer. An agreement is concluded at 20% off.

In a $2.5M per-year deal, you have just paid the customer $500,000 per year for as long as they remain a customer, just for asking for a discount. When they desire to buy more from you, you can bet they will be asking for more discounts as well.

While I wasn't exactly sure what I wanted to do, I knew these two strategies did not feel right. Our pricing model was missing something: the buyer's confidence.

THE "SOME SOUND BASIS" PROBLEM

> The knowledge of buyers has increased, and they are no longer disposed to pay what is asked of them, unless persuaded in their minds that the sellers regulate their prices on some sound basis.
>
> —Thomas Herbert Russell,
> *Salesmanship: Theory and Practice*, 1910

When grocery shopping, there is a reason why you don't walk up to the cashier with your loaf of bread, bag of tomatoes, and container of sliced ham and say, *"Due to budget constraints, in order for me to move forward, I am going to need a discount."* You don't walk into a clothing store, pull up to the gas station, or patronize a restaurant and ask for a discount. In each instance, the representative at said business will tell you the price is the price. If you can't afford it, don't buy it . . . or buy less of it.

Why? Because the price, in your mind, is based on "some sound basis." The price has been predetermined. You don't know how, but you assume the price is the price; take it or leave it.

The business-to-business world has a "some sound basis" problem.

The assumption that your price is not the best price has been built over many years of experience by many buyers. Every single day, we reinforce the idea that our price could be better through the subtle words and actions we communicate with our prospects and customers.

Picture this: It is a cold, rainy day, but your dog needs to be walked. There's a path behind your home where you walk your dog daily, but today, given the weather, you plan to speed through it. You put the dog on his leash and head out.

Once on the path, your dog pulls you off to complete his business. As you stand awkwardly waiting, you see a rock with a piece of paper peeking out from under it. Curious, you kick over the rock to see what's on this piece of paper. It's not just a piece of paper. It's a $20 bill. What do you do?

First, you likely look around, thinking to yourself, *Can I keep this?*

Second, your priorities of speed, warmth, and dryness have just taken a back seat. This free money under a random rock has changed your focus. Now, the walk just became potentially more valuable. You think, *If there's a $20 bill under this rock, where else should I be looking?*

Third, you begin to crisscross the path, kicking over every branch and rock that may have money hiding under it.

The minute we give away anything for free in our deals is similar to what has just happened on the path. Your customer's brain has just been prompted into thinking, *Wow, that was easy. What else can I ask for?*

The customer asks for a discount, and we give in. "Would a 10% discount work?"

Then the customer asks to pay more slowly, asking for monthly terms instead of annual, or NET60 terms instead of NET30, and we reply affirmatively. *"We can't do NET60, but how does NET45 sound?"*

While it may feel like you're doing yourself, your organization, and the customer a favor, you have triggered their brains into a feeling that "some sound basis" does not exist. You've triggered your customer into slowing down, crisscrossing the path to finalizing your deal, and eroding the short-term and long-term value of this customer.

You might be thinking, *Why not just say no? Why not tell them that our price is our price, and they can take it or leave it?*

While you could certainly draw a hard line, the truth is that there are things valuable to your organization that your customer may be willing to give you in exchange for what they are asking for. There is an opportunity to provide flexibility, build trust, and continue to maintain focus on your customer's desired outcomes through the Four Levers.

THE POWER OF THE REVEAL

When you enter any sort of pricing negotiation, your prospect's organization has called upon the individual you are negotiating with to represent their organization. Think of it almost like a lawyer calling a witness to support an accusation. This quote from Francis L. Wellman's 1903 book *The Art of Cross-Examination* lays the foundation:

> The professional witness is always partisan, ready and even eager
> to serve the party calling him. This fact should be ever present
> in the mind of the cross-examiner . . . Assume that an expert
> witness called against you has come prepared to do you all the

harm he can, and will avail himself of every opportunity to do so which you may inadvertently give him.

The person you are negotiating with is partisan. They walk in only understanding their viewpoint and their interests. It's incumbent upon you, the person guiding the discussion, to, as Wellman puts it, "encourage the witness to betray his partisanship."

How do we do this? By presenting the why. Laying the foundation by presenting our cards faceup. By helping the customer understand what actually drives a business. By helping a customer understand what matters and the trade-offs included in reaching a mutually beneficial outcome. Once their "witness" feels your openness, their desire to maintain their partisanship quickly erodes. Transparency begets transparency.

———

Back to David and Goliath. The light bulb in my brain lit up! To this day, I'm not sure how, but the entire future of my approach to negotiation changed based on the next sentence that came out of my mouth.

While I don't remember the words exactly, the message was this: "You know the four items I wrote on the whiteboard behind you? Maybe we can use those as a path to help you get there. These are the four elements that drive our business. Let's go through them one by one."

1. Volume

The first and primary driver of our pricing model is Volume, or how much stuff you buy. The more products, services, technology, licenses, or whatever solution you commit to purchase, the better. Commit to more = good. Commit to less = bad.

2. Timing of Cash

As it turns out, our company, and every for-profit company in the world, likes money. The faster you pay for the solution, the better. Pay quickly = good. Pay slowly = bad.

3. Length of Commitment

The longer you commit to our products, technology, and services, the better. Long commitments = good. Shorter or no commitment = bad.

4. Timing of the Deal

Predictability is very valuable to our company, and really, to every company on the planet. Your willingness to mutually align with us around the timing of when you will sign, start, and pay = good. Unpredictability = bad.

In the following four chapters, we'll go through each element individually. However, the conversation was simple. The Four Levers became our framework. I explained how their pricing was configured based on each of the four.

And as the discussion progressed, a phrase exited my brain through my mouth, and the vibe of the discussion immediately changed.

"IN THE FORM OF A DISCOUNT"

When providing any concession to a customer—say, a discount—you are paying the customer. If you charge $100 for something and provide a 10% discount, you are giving the customer $10. Instead of having $100, you will now have $90. For what? What are you getting for your $10?

Pointing to the Four Levers on the whiteboard, then discussing the first one, Volume, I explained to the group that these Four Levers are the items we are willing to pay them for "in the form of a discount."

"Pay you in the form of a discount."

This is a phrase that conveys the idea that while our price is our price, there are elements of value that we are able to trade in exchange for what the customer values. A discount is essentially a charitable contribution you are providing to your customer, which only serves to assist their bottom line. You are paying your customer in the form of the concession you are providing. What are you getting in return?

The answer should be either a larger purchase, faster payments, a longer commitment, or a more predictably timed transaction. Let's dig into each element and the conversation that took place, then put it all together for you to make negotiating your deals easier, more valuable, and more predictable, in turn making your upsells and cross-sells more valuable, all while building trust.

CHAPTER 2

The First Lever: Volume

**The expert salesman sells his goods, not the price. He
does not fundamentally sell his goods by his price.
His goods sell the price, not the price the goods.**
—Oscar S. Dorr, 1921

I said, "Let's start with the first lever, Volume. The primary driver of our pricing model is based on how much of our solution you are willing to commit to. Committing to a larger purchase up front is better for us, and is reflected in your pricing. Committing to a smaller purchase up front is obviously not as beneficial for us, and as such, the per-license price will be higher."

What do you sell? Sales have always been measured in terms of Volume—the number of licenses, tires, refrigerators, bowling balls, devices, locations, or even hours. Sometimes Volume is expressed in terms of weight, gallons, bales, or some other standard form of measurement.

When a client is willing to commit to a higher Volume of whatever it is you sell, that's good for you and your organization, right? Buying many is certainly better than if they only want to commit to very few. Given that every for-profit company in the world prefers larger Volume commitments versus smaller ones, it is highly likely that the organization you are selling to rewards their customers when they make larger Volume commitments too.

Over the past 10 months, we had been working primarily within one division of this oil services company. However, they had two additional significant divisions, one of which had shown some interest in bringing on our technology as well.

I said, "The pricing you have before you is based on the total number of licenses [for the one division] you would be committing to."

Like many companies, our pricing already followed a tiered model. Buy more licenses, and the price per license goes down. In the first of the many jokes I nervously delivered that landed with a thump, I added, "Based on the number of licenses you are purchasing, you have already earned a 15% discount versus just purchasing a few licenses at a time. So we're nearly halfway there!"

Barely cracking a smile, their procurement leader clarified, "Okay, but we need a 35% discount from where the pricing is currently."

"I know. I was just . . . well, let's move on."

I explained to the group that if they desired to commit to adding licenses, which would cover the additional division that had shown initial interest, now, "We would pay you for that in the form of a discount." Adding those additional licenses would earn them a per-license price break of 5% on all of the licenses.

Because this was a group from procurement, they were unfamiliar with the discussions with the other division and not aware of their progress, but they were appreciative of the understanding that this relationship could grow beyond the initial contract.

The procurement lead continued: "As we discussed, this first division is anxiously awaiting the completion of this negotiation and agreement so they can get moving with implementation. Knowing how we work internally, our concern would be that to add an additional division to this initial agreement would significantly slow down the process. It would need to be fully scoped. Budget would need to be determined, allocated, and approved. While we appreciate the understanding of this component, we won't be able to add those additional licenses at this time."

"Okay, that makes perfect sense," I said.

APPLICATION

You and your organization desire commitment from your clients, and the larger the commitment, the better for all involved. Thinking about your pricing model, do you have Volume discounts available to your clients? Is there a tiered pricing model where, at different tiers, the pricing is adjusted based on the amount of product, technology, or services the client is committing to? With this first lever, Volume is likely the primary driver of your price. It is incumbent upon you to explain to the client how the Volume commitment works in your organization.

A few years ago, I was on the sales leadership team of the leading provider of email marketing solutions. Thinking about the emails you receive from retailers and brands, it is likely those emails are driven by a vendor like this that helps those retailers set up the email templates, optimize how those emails appear, meet all regulatory requirements, and ensure that they end up in your inbox.

Our pricing was primarily driven by the number of emails you expected to send on an annual basis. The price was based on the acronym CPM, which stands for "cost per mille." (The Latin word *mille* means "a thousand.") Some of our clients quite literally sent millions of emails per year. At the beginning of the contract term, we worked with the client to configure that estimate, and the CPM (cost per thousand emails) was based on that commitment. Commit to a million? Your cost per mille would be less than if you desired to only send out a few thousand emails.

In your world, maybe you are selling licenses, locations, or devices, and can configure your pricing in a way that reflects the Volume commitment. Maybe you are selling services. Can you configure your "per hour" pricing based on a commitment to how many hours of services your client may need? If you are pricing on a "fixed fee" basis, that Volume may reflect how large the project may be.

One of my clients handles events for their clients. They had established pricing based on the event they would be managing, and their primary Volume pricing was based on the size of the audience, the length of the event, and the number of resources that would be required from their organization.

What drives your Volume component? If you do not already have one, establish a tiered pricing model that rewards your customers for committing to more Volume. Pay your customers for larger commitments.

Given their inability to commit to more, we placed an "X" on the whiteboard next to the word *Volume* and moved on to the next lever, the Timing of Cash.

X) Volume 5%

2) Timing of Cash

3) Length of Commitment

4) Timing of the Deal

1) Volume 57

2) Timing of Cash

3) Length of Commitment

4) Timing of the Deal

CHAPTER 3

———

The Second Lever: Timing of Cash

A salesman does not make permanent
friends by yielding to demands for inside
prices. It is a sign of weakness and weakness
excites pity rather than admiration.
—W. N. Aubuchon ("Piccolo"),
Mahin's Magazine, 1904

I said, "As it turns out, we like money. Who knew? The faster you are willing to pay for our products, technology, and services, the better it is for us, and the more we're willing to pay you in the form of a discount."

Consider any aspect of your life where you are trading something in exchange for payment. From the time in elementary school when you had a lemonade stand, you exchanged an ice-cold glass of lemony goodness for the cash. When you go shopping, you pay at the time you receive. There is a penalty for paying later. You could finance the purchase, which has interest associated with it.

Today, if you are a salesperson on a variable compensation plan, I am willing to bet you would prefer your commissions to be paid immediately following a contract being signed with a client, versus waiting a month, a quarter, or even longer than that.

The same mindset is the foundation of every for-profit company. Receiving cash quickly is better than receiving cash slowly, so we set this second lever as the "Timing of Cash."

Back to the conference room. The pricing we had proposed for the multiyear commitment was stated as "up-front, annual payments, NET30." In other words, the proposal identified that this client would pay one annual fee at the beginning of each of the three years during the contract period. At the beginning of the first year of the agreement, they would pay $2.5M, then again at the beginning of Year 2, and again at the beginning of Year 3. The client would pay those invoices NET30, which means payment is due 30 days from invoice issuance.

Given those payment terms, you may think, *Ummm, you have already proposed an up-front payment of NET30. How would you drive the client to pay any faster than that?*

First, remember that while every successful company seeks to collect payments faster rather than slower, every successful company also seeks to hold on to their money for a longer period of time. In other words, we have to set this lever. Your clients will try to pay slower than what you have proposed.

Second, it was still possible to accelerate their payments given the multiyear commitment. My company was still what many might consider a start-up. At this point in our existence, we were still spending more than we were earning as an organization, and eventually, we would run out of cash and need to seek further investment.

Out of my brain popped these words: "The pricing you have before you is based on up-front annual payments with NET30 payment terms. Given that this is a three-year commitment, there is value in our ability to receive the out-years up front as well. If you are willing to pay for Year 2 up front along with Year 1, we will pay you for that in the form of a 5% discount. If you are willing to pay for both Year 2 and Year 3 up front along with Year 1, we are willing to pay you for that in the form of a 10% discount."

The team in the room looked at each other, not saying a word. Again, the total value of the agreement we were negotiating with them, while seven figures, was likely a small purchase for such a massive organization.

Fred spoke up. "Well, that's interesting. I'm not sure how that works. Any of you know?" he said as he looked at his peers around the room. "Can one of you reach out to finance and see how that would work?"

They loved the idea of paying for the entire agreement up front. We loved the idea of having our clients fund our business versus having to find investors, dilute each share of the business, and have the added pressure that goes along with seeing your cash balance slowly decrease each month.

Consider how you propose the timing of payment to your prospects and customers. As we will explore later, on the selling end of a transaction, you would always prefer faster payments. On the buying end, most would typically prefer to pay slowly.

While a few days here or there may not seem to matter to your organization, and while you may feel that accelerated payments do not impact the size or timing of your commission check, you must set this lever! Always.

Similar to the story of finding a $20 bill under a rock while walking your dog, your client is walking along the negotiation path with you. If, in their minds, they believe your pricing and terms are based on something sound, their desire is to finish the process and move on with their lives quickly.

However, the moment a client asks you to pay slower—say, NET60 payment terms versus your proposed NET30—and you reply, *"Would you be okay with NET45?"* you have signaled to the buyer that what you proposed is not based on anything solid. Fifteen days longer to pay may seem like nothing to you or your organization, but in the mind's eye of the client, it's like that $20 bill hiding under a rock. All they had to do was know which rocks to kick over. Now, their process begins with searching for additional easy ways to pay you a little more slowly.

Set the lever.

"Your price is partially based on the Timing of Cash, or in this case, up-front annual payments. NET30," I told them.

Today, with my own business, I clearly establish that part of my pricing model is based on aligning payment to program delivery. Lever set. Not a week goes by when a client isn't trying to sneak slower payment terms into an agreement. Unless the lever has been set, it can often become the first slow leak in your deal value.

We offered to pay them in the form of a discount in exchange for their willingness to pay us faster. They agreed. We put a big check mark on the whiteboard next to "2. Timing of Cash." It was time to move on to the third lever.

X) Volume 5%

☆ Timing of Cash 10%

3) Length of Commitment

4) Timing of the Deal

1) Volume $V
2) Timing of Cash $C
3) Length of Commitment
4) Timing of the Deal

CHAPTER 4

The Third Lever: Length
of Commitment

The customer who buys an article where
the price has been cut is not nearly so loyal,
nor has he the confidence in the house,
than the man who pays full price.
—Nilas Oran Shively, Salesmanship, 1916

At this point in the discussion, I noticed an amazing shift in the vibe of the room. When Fred first opened the conference room doors, it felt as though we were walking into a coliseum. Two separate sides, prepared to do battle. Well, in this case, one side was prepared to do battle, and one side (us) was feeling as though we were about to be beaten and bloodied.

However, writing the Four Levers on the board put our cards faceup on the table. We had begun the discussion by sharing the levers that drove our business and our pricing model. There was a mutual under-standing of the structure by which the pricing would be negotiated.

There was no more adversarial vibe, vendor versus customer. Instead, there were eight people sitting around a table discussing how we would mutually come to an agreement where our businesses would be leaving with an outcome commensurate with our goals.

It was almost as if our "adversaries" couldn't wait to talk about the third lever!

"A core tenet of our pricing is a commitment to our products, technology, and services. The longer you commit to our solutions, the better it is for us, and the more we are willing to pay you in the form of a discount."

The pricing on the table was based on a three-year commitment to our solutions, based on how much Volume they were committing to (the first lever), and based on up-front annual payments to be paid NET30 (the second lever).

I explained to the customer how any commitment allows us to plan and resource our business. The longer the commitment, the better we are able to plan, and as such, the better their price would be.

I said, "If you are willing to lengthen your commitment, that's valu-able to us. If you are willing to extend your commitment out to four years, we are willing to pay you in the form of a 5% discount. Extend out to five years, another 5% discount is available. In other words, extending this agreement from a three-year to a five-year commitment would result in a 10% discount."

The group discussed this concept almost as though David and I weren't even in the room.

Fred chimed in, "That's an interesting idea. However, given the unpredictability of our industry, committing to anything for even three years is a challenge. Extending this out to five years would likely be dif-ficult, but we can put a question mark next to that one for now while we inquire about the possibility."

APPLICATION

Thinking about your pricing and your business, is there a different price for a client who commits month-to-month versus one who commits annually? There should be. Is there value to your business in having the predictability that comes with a client willing to tell you in writing that they do not intend to throw you out for a specified period? Is there value to your business when that client is willing to tell you they will not be leaving for one, three, or even five-plus years?

Many companies I work with simply throw out a commitment without an explanation: *"Our pricing is based on a two-year commitment."*

Meanwhile, the client's subconscious brain is shouting, *So what?*

It is imperative that, with each lever, you are prepared to explain the "why." Why does commitment matter? When considering a proposal, the client needs to understand clearly the value that is received for a commitment and how that is already reflected in the pricing. In the case above, we made it clear that the pricing they had before them was based on a three-year commitment. A one-year commitment would cost more; a five-year commitment would cost less.

As such, it is also important to consider the Length of Commitment that makes sense for the client, not just something that makes you feel good. It would be ridiculous to propose to a client, *"Our pricing is based on a 20-year commitment. If you want a shorter commitment, it'll cost you!"* Take it easy.

If you're selling a piece of software, and that software requires time to implement and configure while it also has a long tail of value to both you and the client, explain it—especially if you are winding the implementation effort into the cost of the annual commitment. For instance: *"Our pricing is based on a two-year commitment to our products and services. This is partially based on the up-front investment we make to ensure you are up and running quickly and seeing the results right away."*

CUSTOMER PERCEPTION OF RISK

Remember, the organizations you are selling to are also motivated by these same levers, but the buyer is motivated to do the opposite: commit to a little, hold on to cash, and have the ultimate flexibility to get out whenever they want.

In other words, the longer a customer is asked to commit, the more risk they feel in making such a commitment. Here in the United States, I have a contract with Verizon for my mobile phone needs. My price is based on a two-year contract. If I want a shorter commitment, the price would be higher. I need to feel comfortable that, given my needs, the odds I would want to change providers within two years are small.

What you are asking for is a commitment to your products, solutions, and services for a predictable period of time given the contracted assumption that your solutions do what you have represented them to do. And you are offering to pay them in the form of a discount or concession in exchange for doing so.

Standing at the whiteboard, I placed a question mark next to the third lever. That question mark later became an X, as they confirmed afterward that they would not be able to extend the commitment beyond three years.

X) Volume 5%

☆ Timing of Cash 10%

X) Length of Commitment 10%

4) Timing of the Deal

CHAPTER 5

The Fourth Lever: Timing of the Deal

SELL the right goods, at the right price, in
the right spirit—and all the forces of good
in the universe will be pulling for you.
—*Matthew Sales*, Specialty
Salesman Magazine, 1921

I then said to the group, "There is tremendous value in our ability to predict our business. If you are willing to help us forecast when this will get done, that mutual alignment is valuable to us, and something we're willing to pay you for in the form of a discount."

The delivery of this fourth lever, the "Timing of the Deal," should sound different from what so many organizations do today. Every organization has a responsibility to predict its own ability to invest in the right areas of the business and to assign and allocate resources, for both its investors' sanity and its own. That's valuable to your business, so pay the customer to help you forecast.

DITCH THE FAKE EXPIRING DISCOUNT

"25% off everything—ends TONIGHT!"

"Final Hours: 40% off."

"Best deal ever's final countdown—20% off!"

"Two days only . . . 50% off!"

When you sign up for a retailer's promotional emails, what is the common theme of those communications? It is likely a widely used technique called the fake expiring discount. It's designed to create browsing interest and a sense of urgency to make an immediate purchase.

However, there is an irony to the use of this technique, both in retail environments and in business-to-business communication:

1. The fake expiring discount signals to the buyer that the purchase price is not what was originally proposed.
2. It signals that the seller can afford to part with the product for less than the list price, regardless of when it is purchased.
3. Ironically, in many cases, the fake expiring discount causes a buyer to wait, not accelerate their purchase.

A few Novembers ago, I managed to mangle one of my favorite sweaters. It's a merino crewneck sweater from Banana Republic that I accidentally threw in the wash with the rest of my clothes . . . washed, dried, unwearable. So, off to bananarepublic.gap.com to buy another.

As the weather turned cooler, everything was lined up for me to buy. I wanted to purchase a new sweater. It was not the most expensive sweater around, so I had the funds to make the purchase. When I visited the website, I found the exact same sweater available in my size. Yet I did not immediately make the purchase. I waited.

Why? Because I knew a discount was coming. In mid-November, I knew the list price of the sweater was not the best price I could get. While I could not be sure when the sweater would go on sale, Banana Republic has deep sales all the time. And, seeing as Black Friday, the biggest shopping day of the year in the United States, was approaching, which coincides with the biggest sales of the year, paying full price for the sweater felt like I would be flushing dollars down the toilet. So I waited.

Sure enough, the inevitable deep discounts arrived. I purchased my favorite sweater for 40% off. Instead of creating urgency, anticipating a discount caused me to do the opposite.

Since the beginning of time, in the business-to-business world, we have taught our buyers to wait for a discount. Whether we are approaching the end of the quarter or year, or just creating some incentive a sales leader believes will drive lower-margin revenue to hit a target, discounts are always on the horizon. Buyers do not always know exactly when, but they know a discount is coming if they just wait long enough.

We have unwittingly taught our buyers that waiting for a discount is the best policy, even though they may be ready to buy.

As a sales leader, you may feel like you are giving your salespeople a gift when you work with your CEO or CFO to get approval to communicate a quarter-end discount to your prospects. Especially in an environment where you are not just selling transactional products but more complex enterprise-level solutions, the thought is often that the earlier the promotion is established in the customer's mind, the better.

But, in fact, the quarter-end discount communication is doing the opposite. If it is the middle of the quarter, and you tell your customer,

"Hey, we are offering an extra incentive to bring in business this quarter. In exchange for your signature this quarter, we are offering an extra 10% off," you have just told your customer two things:

1. The proposed price is not the actual price. While the vendor has communicated that the price is based on a signature in the current quarter, the proposed price is 10% higher than what the customer will actually be paying, regardless of when they sign.
2. The quarter-end is important; thus, waiting until the quarter-end nears and then asking for more would be in the prospect's best interest.

As a result, the prospects have now been subconsciously signaled to wait and then ask for more. *If they're already offering 10%, I'll bet I can get more if I slow-play this a bit and simply ask.*

Our quarter-end discounts, based on an arbitrary, made-up date, have eroded your deal values and created a steeper end-of-quarter "hockey stick."

The "hockey stick" refers to the common issue organizations face, where their sales performance over the period of a quarter resembles the shape of a hockey stick. Slow sales took place over the first two and a half months of a quarter with a sudden spike right at the end of it. Higher stress for both you and your organization's sleep effectiveness, higher usage of Advil or your headache-reducing medication of choice, and higher risk.

Risk: Subconsciously incentivizing your customer to wait adds time to your deal's cycle length, and the more time, the higher the risk. Every day a buyer waits is a day when another priority, another option, a job change . . . something else could cause your deal to just go POOF, and disappear.

WHAT TO DO INSTEAD

Pay your customer to help you forecast.

Reading the first paragraph of this chapter again, you may notice something different about how alignment on timing can be set up. It involves *mutual* alignment along with a deeper explanation of the *why* behind it. It takes a little more foundation laying and forethought, but when it is done correctly, you'll find your deal predictability goes up, your perpetual discounting goes down, and your customers are more willing to engage you as their deal guide versus a gross, pressure-inducing salesperson trying to jam a deal into a single-sided desired date.

In my negotiation in Houston, the customer had indicated a desire to finalize the negotiations so the division seeking the solution could begin working toward achieving its desired outcome.

I explained, "There is value to us and our organization in our ability to predict our business. As you can imagine, our ability to forecast impacts every element of our business—especially us personally in sales. Predictability not only helps us with forecasting our business overall, but we also need to be able to predict when and how many resources we will need to be available to begin the work.

"If you are willing to mutually *align around when you think you'll get this done, we're willing to pay you in the form of a discount to stick to it."*

The word *mutually* is so important here. We are no longer throwing out a date and hoping they can scramble their processes to meet it. Instead, we ask them to tell us, and in exchange for sticking to it, we are willing to pay for that predictability.

This meeting was taking place in July. I asked a question that, in hindsight, was probably not the best way to frame it: "From the time we finalize the structure of this agreement, how long do you think it will take you to finalize and sign it?"

The group looked around at one another without an answer. None of them could be sure. Fred spoke up. "Our procurement organization can be unpredictable. It could take two weeks. It could take six weeks. So much depends on things potentially outside of our control."

I replied, "Okay. It is July. Six weeks would take us out to the end of August. Do you think an end-of-August target is a date you could align around?"

They looked around again with uncertainty. "I hope so, but I've seen it take eight or more weeks."

I added, "So, it sounds like September would be the most reasonable time to rally around. Knowing that is of tremendous value to us and our organization. If you are willing to help us with our forecast and get this signed by the end of September, we are willing to pay you a 5% discount to hold to it."

They lit up. "Sign us up for that! If we are still working on this at the end of September, something has gone wrong. We will ensure this gets done in exchange for that discount."

Mutual alignment.

Skin in the game for the client.

Nothing is given without something received.

Our transparency and full explanation for the *why* around the need to forecast accuracy resonated with the group. This was not a desperate attempt to pad our quarter. Instead, they understood the value of predictability to our organization. They understood exactly what we were paying them in the form of a 5% discount. In their minds, they are giving us forecast accuracy. We are ensuring they will be better prepared to kick off this project. We are paying them in the form of a discount to help with both of those elements.

We were mutually aligned around the timing. They contributed to the prediction. And as an added bonus, our transparency begot their transparency. This conversation opened them up to sharing what steps they would have to take following our meeting. We were able to sketch our mutual action plan together.

A big star was written on the whiteboard next to the fourth lever, the Timing of the Deal. We moved on to confirm the discussion around the Four Levers and wrap up the meeting.

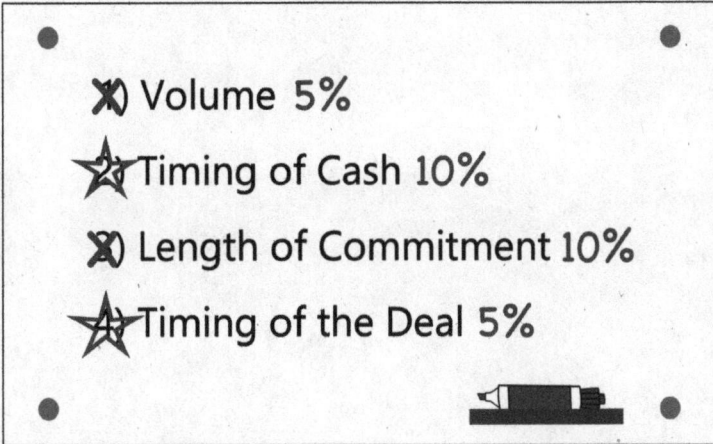

X) Volume 5%

☆ Timing of Cash 10%

X) Length of Commitment 10%

☆ Timing of the Deal 5%

Meeting Wrap . . . and an Accidental Negotiation Framework

If the truth won't sell it, don't sell it.
—*Arthur Dunn*, Scientific Selling
and Advertising, 1922

These Four Levers represent the four ways our pricing is built. If we need to go deeper, the path is here within them, but that's up to you," I said.

They understood.

They expressed an appreciation for the collaborative nature of the discussion. David and I walked out of the room and out of the building almost confused as to what had just happened. There was no arguing. There were no "techniques," no word art, no looking for eye twitches and nervous tapping. It was just pure, cards-faceup alignment.

A young, brand-new sales leader had walked into a multibillion-dollar, 90-year-old oil services company. I was anticipating a conversation with one individual about a multimillion-dollar transaction. I knew him, and I expected that we would have an informal conversation to finalize the terms. Instead, I walked into the lion's den. They brought their might, and I accidentally accomplished everything we could have hoped for: an agreement on the pricing terms, a balanced transaction that both parties could feel good about, enhanced trust instead of erosion, and a foundation for every transaction that would take place between the parties from that day forward.

It felt good. It was easy. I started writing down what had happened because if negotiating could be that easy, I wanted to mechanize it.

It didn't work because I was a sales leader. It worked because it is the truth. This approach is simple and is meant to empower you, regardless of your role, to handle negotiations on your own. You will no longer have to "*take this back to my boss*," or "*justify this to my CFO*" (which, if we are being honest, are comments that aren't very truthful most of the time anyway). You've got it.

In this negotiation, the procurement team communicated a need to slash 35% of the price from the contract. Instead of arguing about the value, instead of playing pretend with these professional buyers about what we could and could not do, the Four Levers established the rules.

Our price, as well as your price, and the price of every for-profit company in the world, is based on four things:

1. Volume: How much the customer buys from you.
2. Timing of Cash: How fast the customer pays you.
3. Length of Commitment: How long the customer commits to you.
4. Timing of the Deal: Alignment around when the customer signs.

Buy more. Pay faster. Commit longer. Help us predict. That's it.

We offered this group a path to reduce their dollar investment by 5% in exchange for accelerating the commitment to an additional division of their organization, which they were not prepared to do.

We offered this group a path to reduce their dollar investment by 10% in exchange for accelerating both their second- and third-year payment to up-front (5% for each year) NET30. They obliged.

We offered this group a path to reduce their dollar investment by 10% in exchange for committing to two additional years, from a three-year commitment to a five-year commitment (5% for each year), which they were not prepared to do.

We offered this group a path to reduce their dollar investment by 5% in exchange for their willingness to help us predict the timing of when they would sign, and when they would be ready to proceed with the project. It was their *mutual* commitment, based on their ability to formalize the agreement, not an arbitrary fake expiring discount. They obliged.

The meeting ended. We left that room as friends. We didn't give anything away for free, and it was easy. There was no grandstanding. And, more importantly, for every dollar we did give away in the form of a concession, we received something of value in return. They received 15% off of their investment. For our payment of 10%, we received accelerated cash. Instead of them paying $2.5M in Year 1, then us waiting for another $2.5M in 12 months, followed by another $2.5M in 24 months, we received a wire transfer of $6.4M immediately. This included our payment of 5% in exchange for forecastability. We received *firm* forecastability based on their commitment, not our made-up timeline, or artificial attempts to create urgency. They told us when they would sign, and we explained clearly how we were paying them in the form of a discount to hold to it.

While that may sound impossible—pie in the sky, cotton candy, and unicorns—of course, things happened after we left. They had requests.

They asked for other things. Each time, the Four Levers became the foundation for addressing those requests, as nearly every request fit squarely into one of them.

Let's explore how to prevent as many of those requests and demands as possible. Then, we will examine each of the most common issues with an approach you can use.

CHAPTER 6

Positioning Your Price

> The special discount, or the cut price, given
> without a good reason is a closing method
> that is full of danger. In a great many cases the
> salesman hurts rather than helps his house and
> could get his price and maintain the respect of
> his employer by holding out for the price that he
> should get. The situation is that salesmen have
> taught buyers in many lines to expect the price
> to be cut, no matter what figure is quoted.
> —The Salesman's Handbook, I.C.S. (International
> Correspondence Schools), 1924

Have you ever run a marathon? I have not. I typically do my best running while being chased, but that is beside the point.

For those who have run a marathon, it is safe to assume that they did not wake up one morning, look outside, and think, *Wow, what a beautiful day. I should go for a run.* Then, realizing there's a marathon nearby, think, *Hey, that looks like fun! I've got new shoes. I'm gonna head over there and give it a try.* Those individuals might be dead by the halfway point.

A marathon is an *event*. It is something that takes place on a day and a time. But more importantly, it is a *process* that begins way before the day and time of the event. Marathon runners begin preparing months ahead of time, building a foundation to be able to withstand the punishment their bodies will take running a 26.2-mile (42.2 km) race. While a runner may be able to complete a marathon without the process beginning months ahead of time, the event tends to be most successful when there's a foundation.

Similarly, a negotiation is an event as well. Under most circumstances, there is a conversation or a meeting that takes place, likely at the end of the sales cycle, where pricing and terms are negotiated and finalized. While the story of my Houston negotiation mirrors what one might imagine being in a marathon with no preparation would be like, it still went really well. However, a pricing and terms negotiation can run even more smoothly when that foundation is laid during the initial conversations with the prospective customer.

SET EXPECTATIONS EARLY

When do you set pricing expectations for your clients? Earlier in my career, the popular philosophy was to wait to discuss price. This philosophy has withstood any logical reasoning for way too long.

First, when making a purchase, our brains are trying to predict whether or not the "juice will be worth the squeeze." Our brains are attempting to assess whether an outlay of time, resources, and dollars will be worth the return and potential outcome.

Without knowing what that "squeeze" will be in terms of an estimated range, our brains cannot properly file the value of the "juice."

Imagine you are considering buying a new car but aren't allowed to see the price until the salesperson shows you the car of your dreams. Or imagine you're buying a new microwave online, but they hide the price until after you have read about all of the features. There is a reason why every online store has the price boldly listed next to the product—so you can access the value against the cost. The equation requires it.

In a 2020 study in the *Journal of Marketing Research*,[3] researchers confirmed that "information symmetry in the front end has made it easier to build trust" and that "building trust is arguably the primary objective of negotiators." The research also showed that customers buy more on the back end when salespeople are transparent about their pricing on the front end. Up-front transparency on the price, along with how it is determined, is the key connector to successful negotiation outcomes.

In other words, sharing the estimated investment that will be required, along with the levers that determine the price, is vital to avoiding many of the problems that come up during the buying process. There's power to up-front expectation setting.

Conversely, not sharing a pricing range can have detrimental negative impacts on the sales relationship, the sale itself, and the long-term value of each customer.

Think about a time when you have had a feeling of sticker shock. The *Britannica Dictionary* defines it as "a feeling of surprise and disappointment caused by learning that something you want to buy is very expensive." Nothing in that definition sounds positive, does it? Yet, organizations and their salespeople have treated concealing the price as some sort of valid selling technique for a hundred years.

Take the reality television series *Property Brothers*, for example. First appearing on the W Network in Canada and eventually picked up by the

HGTV channel in the United States,[4] two brothers, Jonathan and Drew Scott, work with couples and individuals to find their dream homes. However, the potential home buyers are essentially "shocked" into wanting to renovate their existing home versus buying a new one. In a typical episode, the brothers interview a couple desiring a new home.

"Tell us what you'd like to see in a new home."

The couple replies, "Well, we really want a four-bedroom home. Oh, and a big backyard for the kids and our dog, Fluffy. It would be great if it were close to town so we can walk to a coffee shop. Amazing schools are a must."

"And what's your budget?"

"$750,000," they reply.

Next, the Scott brothers show the couple a home that matches their desires. "This house has everything. See, over the backyard's fence, you can see the coffee shop right there."

The couple is drooling. They have found their dream home.

"How much is this house?" the couple asks.

"$1.3M."

The couple is floored. They are angry. "Why would you show us this house?" they ask.

The brothers use this technique to shock the couple into wanting to just renovate their existing home. "You can't afford the things you want. But we can give you most everything you want by simply fixing up your current home." The couple is disappointed, reluctantly engaging in the renovation project.

While the show ran for 14 seasons, in not one episode did the couple say, *"Oh, okay. Well, if that's how much it costs, we'll find the money!"* Instead, the couples spend time being upset by the thought that they will never be able to afford their dream homes.

While value matters, your buyers aren't operating in a vacuum like they may be on a TV show. Buyers have budgets, constraints, and competing priorities. An extended value pitch while intentionally avoiding the setting of any pricing expectation assumes a buyer will stretch to pay anything for perceived value, which simply isn't true. If the pricing ends up being wildly out of range, you have wasted everyone's time.

Start by setting a range . . . an expectation they can begin to understand. And do it during the first meeting.

How? Like this: *"Based on our understanding of your environment so far and our work with clients like yours, your investment for a solution like this will likely be between $X and $Y. We may be off, as this is based on a number of assumptions, which we will hone in on during the process."*

Then, the key question: *"If this range is way off of your expectations, can we talk about it now versus later?"*

Then, get ready to listen.

First, if you are talking about a six- or seven-figure solution to a four- or five-figure buyer (or vice versa), one of you is in the wrong conversation. Find that out right now. Your unexpected honesty disarms the customer, builds trust, and most importantly, allows you to qualify whether there is mutual value in continuing the conversation.

Second, the customer is now better able to access the value against an expected investment.

Now, if your solution is premium priced, it's worth sharing that up front. Again, win fast by building trust, but lose the deals you are going to lose anyway—fast.

How? Like this: *"There are less expensive alternatives in the market. As we proceed through the journey together, there is a reason why our customers invest in our solutions as they do, and our expectation is that you will see why. However, if that level of investment is far from your expectations, it may be best if we either part ways now or strategize a path to preparing for such an investment."*

By having this conversation early, you have either (a) protected the most valuable piece of inventory you can convert to revenue—your time—or (b) you have set an expectation that disarms your competition. We will discuss this more later in the book, but it seems as though every company I work with has one or two competitors willing to discount their way to a win or, in some more aggressive cases, simply "buy business" with loss-leader pricing. "Any revenue is good revenue" in competitors' minds doesn't help you when you've invested your precious inventory of time into an opportunity only to lose it for a silly reason right at the end. Setting the proper range, and teeing up the fact that there are lower-priced alternatives, disarms that conversation quickly.

Your alternative is to lose slowly or be forced to discount heavily.

Sharing the Four Levers

When discussing range of pricing, there is an opportunity to educate your potential customer a little on how the pricing will be configured. Set the foundation for the negotiation. When considering the range, share with the customer, "*We price based on the number of (products, hours, licenses, locations, etc.) you need.*" The first lever, Volume, is the primary way pricing is determined. Share it: "*There are tiers based on the commitment level, which we'll discuss later.*"

Then, communicate the second and third levers immediately as a part of the discussion: "*Our pricing model is based on annual, up-front payments [Timing of Cash] and a commitment to the solution for a period of one year [Length of Commitment].*"

You have now laid the foundation for three of the Four Levers. The pricing is based on how much they buy (Volume), how fast they pay (Timing of Cash), and how long they commit (Length of Commitment).

Because you are early in the engagement with the client, holding off on sharing the fourth lever (Timing of the Deal) is recommended, primarily because gaining the greatest benefit from the fourth lever requires *mutual* alignment around timing. Unless you run a very short sales cycle where the client is in a position to accurately predict their own procurement cycle and can truly give you an accurate estimate on when they would be ready to sign, saving this lever for later is the best policy.

NO NEED TO "WAIT FOR POWER"

Think about the Thomas Herbert Russell "some sound basis" quote from page 12. Your price is your price, with levers allowing your buyers the flexibility to adjust the price based on the elements that maintain the integrity of your business and your other customers.

"But, Todd, shouldn't we wait until we talk to the ultimate buyer before we share the price?"

If your price is your price, and the levers are the levers, you can share your pricing with anyone within your prospect's organization that you want to. There is no reason to wait until you're speaking to someone who can buy. When done confidently, the following happens:

1. **Confidence is contagious:** When we deliver a message of price without confidence, we signal to the buyer that we are either unsure of the price, or we are worried the customer will be blown off their chair. Confidence cannot be faked. With a conviction that your price is your price, based on the levers, your customer will feel it. They'll become confident in you and your solution.

2. **Better qualification IN or OUT:** As mentioned above, by delivering the range in conjunction with the framework for how the pricing is determined and can be adjusted, you are better able to "qualify" whether this prospect or customer is able to carry the baton for you in the organization, and you are better able to have the confidence that your valuable asset of time is being spent in the right places.

3. **Improved navigation:** When describing the range and the pricing model, if your contact is not able to procure at the required level of investment, they are often able to include those in an organization who can.

4. **They'll remember:** When the foundation is set through the levers, when it comes time to negotiate, your customer will have the tools to negotiate their own deal.

The foundation is set. The discussions proceed. Now, let's reinforce the levers again when it is time to formally deliver the price, in the form of a proposal.

CHAPTER 7

Proposals

> The purchasing agent looks upon every man
> or woman who comes to sell him goods with
> suspicion. Self-preservation is the first law of life.
> The salesman can either help him or hurt him.
> Therefore, until he is made to feel otherwise,
> he occupies the position of antagonist.
> —*Elizabeth Z. Toth, Salesology Magazine, 1924*

When a prospective customer asks you for a proposal, what are they really asking for?

Put yourself in the shoes of the customer you are selling to. If you are selling anything that requires multiple stakeholders on the customer's side to reach a consensus, the individual who's asking you for a proposal is asking for three things:

1. **An internal sales tool:** Your customer needs something they can use that will theoretically help them assemble their internal sales pitch.

2. **A prediction:** You have had conversations with your customer. Maybe you have presented some slides, demonstrated your product, and you have made a number of claims and pitches as to what your solution can and cannot do. Unless your customer is an expert in shorthand and captured every word, they need something they can digest to align with their understanding. *Will this solution address the outcomes I hope to achieve?* The proposal should also serve as a prediction of the journey.

3. **CYA:** In many cases, the customer is looking for a "cover your a**" document, where, in writing, there is documented language that substantiates the claims you have made during the interactions you have had or will have.

With those three items in mind, when your customer receives a proposal, what page do they flip to first? While context, situation, and the proposal recipient matter, it is commonly estimated that anywhere from 60% to 80% of proposal recipients immediately skip to the *pricing* page first.

~~NEVER~~ ALWAYS SEND A PROPOSAL WITHOUT REVIEWING IT "LIVE" WITH THE CUSTOMER

I was originally taught, and continue to hear this advice, that we should never just send over a proposal. Any price or plan must be delivered and explained "live" in person. Or, at the very least, make sure you have a call scheduled shortly after the proposal is sent.

Years ago, I would have agreed with this advice. The live discussion delivers context along with the proposal . . . so it's not just words on pages and the prospect is able to understand how best to consume and understand it. And through your discussion, theoretically, you can control the flow of how they consume the information so the *value* is firmly defined before consuming the *price*.

However, put yourself in the recipient of the proposal's position. Having to receive and review a proposal via a live discussion adds friction to their process and evaluation. In other words, it is annoying to have to schedule a call to review a proposal. Remember that the customer is trying to predict whether the juice will be worth the squeeze in moving forward with you. In other words, *"Will our expenditure of time, resources, effort, and dollars be worth the outcomes we expect to receive in making a purchase?"* The customer wants their questions answered in their order as quickly as possible. It is why e-commerce works so well, with all the answers available in one place, consumable when and how desired. A conversation and live walk-through slows the process for the buyer, providing more opportunities for other options or priorities to derail your opportunity.

In a consensus sale (i.e., one with multiple decision-makers), the buyer must share the proposal internally. That may mean she will have to schedule internal calls or use valuable time during team meetings. She will need to be the salesperson for you without you in the room. This begins the telephone game of consensus buying, where the value and message get muddled over time.

In years past, the only alternative to sharing the proposal "live" was to send the proposal, cross your fingers, say a little prayer, and then stare at your email inbox or phone and wait for feedback. While full of anxiety for the salesperson, this approach is the ultimate in ease and friction removal for the buyer. They can consume the information on their own schedule, skip right to the sections they care about, and gloss over the things that don't apply. During a "live" delivery, they have to sit through the pitch again and wait for the price and actualization information they're really most interested in.

Also, it's a fast path to their needed answers. In the decision-making process, the faster we can get to "What's the price?"; "What will this look like in our world?"; and "What will I need to do to prepare our organization?" the more likely it is to happen. When we wait to get our internal picture configured, other priorities sneak their way in.

The Best of Both Worlds: Send a Video

However, the downside is the customer now has little context for the words on the pages. The buyer often doesn't know how best to consume the proposal and is left to figure it out independently, which is inherently more work. Decisions sometimes get made based on an inaccurate perception of the words they're reading. And, with no context, their consensus-building efforts become harder, too, as the message they deliver internally may not be the right one.

But there is a way you can do both the summarization homework for the buyer and be in the room when she's building consensus without actually being in the room.

While I hope there are many ideas you can take from this book, if you really want to stand out, aid your customer in their internal selling process, provide context, save time, and speed decision-making, try this:

1. **Finalize your proposal and prepare it for delivery.**
2. **Using video technology, RECORD yourself walking through the proposal very briefly.** Keep the proposal on the main part of the screen and your face taking them through the context and pricing. Keep it brief, no more than four to seven minutes long.

A few years ago, I spoke with the CEO of a $100M+ consulting firm in Chicago. It wasn't a discovery or qualification call; it was simply an informal discussion that almost accidentally progressed to discussing the possibility of me providing sales training and consulting to his partners. The conversation ended with him saying, "Todd, can you send me over a write-up or proposal, along with your pricing? I will socialize it with our partners and business development leader, and then we'll want to schedule another couple of calls to hone in on what we want to do."

I put together an eight-page proposal, which started with a recommended approach; a description of the programs I would suggest; how those programs would be customized, delivered, and reinforced; and the pricing model. Along with it, using a technology called Ecamm Live, I turned on my camera, went split-screen with the proposal on one side and me speaking on the other, and walked him through it.

"James, thank you for considering me as a potential resource for you and your team. To make this proposal easier to understand and share, here's a little context for the why, how, and how much."

The video was four minutes long.

Two days after sending the proposal and the video, I looked at the view counter on my video hosting site. The video had been viewed 56 times!

Given that this was the first time I had ever taken this approach, I was partially mortified. Was there something embarrassing I did that caused this video to go viral within his organization? Why was this simple video being watched by so many people?

Then I received an email from James.

"Todd, we are good to go. No need to have any more discussions. Let's move forward with your recommendation. Go ahead and send us over an agreement."

After sharing my excitement over the quick decision, I had to ask, "Hey, what happened? Why the quick decision? And, not to be creepy, but I noticed the video I sent over was viewed quite a few times."

He replied, "That video saved me multiple meetings and a ton of time. I shared it with our partners and our business development leader, and they were on board in the four minutes it took them to watch it. They also shared it with their teams to not only get them excited about the programs but also as an example of what they could do to make buying easier for their customers."

The video was the consensus-building tool. It removed the homework he would have had to do on his own, ensured the message was not convoluted, and provided personality.

Oh, and regarding the pricing? There was no negotiation at all. When the pricing is delivered in the context of the Four Levers, delivered with confidence, and delivered with an understanding of how they can configure their price, the process is able to proceed smoothly. They understood, paid, and hired me later to do two more programs that skipped the negotiation as well.

I've been sending video proposals for years now. I am constantly getting text messages, emails, or comments from my prospects-turned-customers saying, *"That video saved me three meetings," "That video told me you would be the easiest person to work with,"* and *"I didn't have to present you to our leaders—you did it, and you weren't even there."*

It's a win for everyone.

How Should the Price Be Presented?

It's never too late to share the Four Levers with your prospect or customer. If you haven't communicated the first three levers verbally to your prospect (again, saving the Timing of the Deal conversation for when you can best and most realistically align around the timing), you haven't missed out on your opportunity to lay the foundation.

In any proposal, a key section is the price. When referring to it as a "key section," I mean that unless your prospect has been told clearly what the price will be, it is likely the first section they will skip to when they open the document. If the prospect shares the proposal with others, you can be sure they are looking for the pricing page first.

Have you ever received a real estate flyer in the mail? Occasionally, a local realtor will send a postcard with the headline "On the Market!" or something similar, exclaiming that a house in the vicinity has just gone up for sale. Beautiful picture on the front of the home. Flip it over, and some of the traits of the home are listed, like the number of bedrooms and bathrooms, the square footage, and maybe even the school district. However, more often than not, the price isn't anywhere to be found. I don't know about you, but for me, it is the first thing I look for. Not that I am looking to move, but if I were to have a friend looking for a home in the area, or if I were simply looking to understand the value of my own home, that is the key element in filing this home into our brains. Are you asking me to call you for the price? Do I have to sit down at my computer and look it up? You are asking your potential prospect to do the homework, and as a result, that postcard immediately enters the recycling bin.

Your pricing should be clear. Easy to find. Easy to understand. The Four Levers gives you the opportunity to structure the simplicity and sound basis of your pricing.

To put it simply, you do not need a big chart with the levers bulleted in some cheesy way. Instead, when you list the price, include these four pieces of information:

1. **The proposed price:** List the dollar amount, but along with it, explain what the price is based on. What is the "Volume" component that drives the price? *"$150,500 per year for 500 user licenses, implementation services, 24/7 support . . ."* adding, *"The per-user price is based on a commitment to 500 licenses. The per-user price increases or decreases based on a larger or smaller up-front commitment."*

Use your own words here. The message should be clear: Commit to more, and the price per unit will be lower. Commit to less, and the price per unit will be higher.

2. **The Timing of Cash:** Include a bullet point, a sentence below your pricing chart, or some other clearly communicated place where payment timing impacts the price that states: *"This pricing is based on up-front annual payments, paid NET30."*

   Again, use your own verbiage. However, it should be clear that any change to the timing of payment impacts the proposed investment.

3. **The Length of Commitment:** Similar to the Timing of Cash, clearly communicate how the commitment length impacts the price. You are likely familiar with pricing pages on websites that clearly identify that committing on an annual basis to a solution lowers the price versus a month-to-month commitment. You are clarifying that in your proposal by adding, *". . . and an annual commitment to the solution."*

   Your price is based on the Volume they commit to, how fast they pay (Timing of Cash), and the Length of Commitment. Even glancing at the pricing page should make it clear how the first three of the Four Levers impact the price.

4. **Timing of the Deal**: As mentioned in chapter 6, I recommend holding off discussing the Timing of the Deal lever at this point in the conversation. Mutual alignment with the client requires that your customer be able to predict with relative accuracy when they would be able to execute the agreement. Sharing this lever too early can cause a customer to make a wildly inaccurate *guess*, which does not help anyone.

   However, adding a sentence that ensures your price can change with your sound basis organizational pricing is important: *"This pricing is based on the then-current price as of (today's date)."*

If your company makes a pricing change, a sentence identifying that the price is unlikely to stay exactly the same in perpetuity is helpful. Having a customer dig up your proposal five years later and say, "Okay, we're ready to go!" hurts.

The foundation is set. Your customer understands your price, how it was determined, and what levers impact their price. This does not mean they won't still come after you for more. In fact, it is time to dig into managing those conversations, and that's what the next several chapters do.

CHAPTER 8

The Negotiation "Event" Framework

**The buyer himself is a salesman, seeking
to sell his money for the best proposition
he can obtain in exchange.**
—*Frederic A. Russell, Textbook
of Salesmanship, 1933*

Walking out of the conference room in Houston felt great, with an entire procurement team, armed for battle, disarmed within the first 10 minutes of the discussion, leaving the room soon after with a mutual understanding, a mutual agreement, and as friends who would continue to invest in one another.

Well, things came up: concession requests, language edits, last-minute needs. The endorphins from negotiation meetings wear off. Even seemingly simple things come up during the progression to signature that must be handled effectively, transparently, and with the integrity of your *sound basis* pricing.

While your company's pricing and business model thrive when your customers buy more (Volume), pay faster (Timing of Cash), commit longer (Length of Commitment), and are willing to help you forecast (Timing of the Deal), when buying, the opposite holds true.

As someone who buys things, wouldn't you prefer to commit to as little as possible, hold on to your money as long as possible, make no commitment, and sign whenever you feel like it? You're a human being, and so is a corporate buyer. As stewards of their organizations, buyers in any position, from procurement professionals to department heads to individuals, all desire to maximize their investment, reduce their costs, and reduce their risk.

How can you respond to a customer who asks for any of the following things, without simply giving in, maintaining their confidence that your price is your price, and without eroding trust?

- "We need the price to come down in order to fit our budget."
- "We require the ability to make monthly payments instead of annual."
- "We need to include an out clause [aka 'Termination for Convenience'] in this agreement."
- "We won't be able to get this signed this month. Will you hold the price until next month?"
- "We pay everyone NET60 instead of NET30."
- "We would like to lower the amount of product we're committing to up front."
- "Before we sign, we would like to do a proof-of-concept first [aka a 'pilot']."

- "We found an alternative solution that is considerably less expensive than yours. Match their price and we're ready to move forward."

Does your heart race a bit reading these? I'm willing to bet that if you have been selling long enough, you have heard every single one of these requests. This is where the power of the Four Levers really takes hold. We will dig into each one of these items in the coming chapters, all founded on a simple way to think about how you respond.

Step One: Be Human
Step Two: Review All Four Levers
Step Three: Discuss Using All Four Levers

STEP ONE: BE HUMAN

When a customer or prospect asks for something, it is incumbent on you to listen and understand what is driving the request. With each response, we will discuss what being a human being sounds like. However, if our goal is to help our customers and our own organization achieve mutually optimal outcomes, discussing the motivations for requests will help you determine how best to aid the customer.

For example, when a customer asks for a discount, ask what drives the request. Is it a budget issue? Is it a perception of value issue? Are there approval thresholds contingent on certain investment levels? When a customer asks to hold the price until the following fiscal period, what is driving the delay? Is someone out on vacation? Is there a concern requiring an extra set of internal discussions? Those answers will help you frame how you use the Four Levers and, ultimately, their impact.

STEP TWO: REVIEW ALL FOUR LEVERS

Teach your brain to constantly review all Four Levers with the customer. Remind them over and over about what drives your pricing model and their proposal. Again, we will review the specifics of each request; however, reinforcing these levers will allow your customers to negotiate their own deals. It empowers your customer to negotiate internally with those who must be involved in a purchase.

For example, when a customer asks for a discount, after being a human in Step One, remind the customer: *"As you may recall, our pricing model and the proposal you have before you is based on Four Levers—Volume, or how much you buy; Timing of Cash, or how fast you pay; Length of Commitment, or how long you commit; and Timing of the Deal, or predictability."*

By doing this, you are framing the discussion that is about to happen. You are giving yourself a moment to think. If you've internalized the Four Levers, they will quickly roll off your tongue. And what becomes even more amazing is that your customers will remember them too.

STEP THREE: DISCUSS USING ALL FOUR LEVERS

The trap salespeople often fall into is trying to solve the request instead of giving the customer the tools to solve it for themselves. So often, salespeople jump to, *"Oh, you need to get the price down? Here are the levers that drive our price [Step Two]. If you can sign next week, we can give you a discount."* No.

Instead, here is where you go through all of the levers again to help the customer negotiate their own deal, mutually.

For example, when a customer asks for a discount, after being a human being in Step One, and then reviewing all Four Levers again in Step Two, you can say, *"Let's go through each one to see where we can find those dollars."* You will then be able to discuss each lever; commit to more Volume, speed your Timing of Cash, extend your Length of Commitment, and/or help predict the Timing of the Deal. Those are all things you should be willing to pay for in the form of a discount.

01	Be Human
02	Review ALL FOUR Levers
03	Discuss Using ALL FOUR Levers

You have internalized the Four Levers. You have discussed the first three early in your conversations with the prospect. You have outlined the first three in your proposal. Now, even if you have not discussed and outlined the levers, let's discuss the application when the customer begins to ask for concessions.

CHAPTER 9

"We Need a Discount"

> It is the manufacturers themselves who have taught
> buyers to look with suspicion upon every quotation
> that is put forth as the company's "best price."
> —Sales Management *magazine*, 1931

No matter how well you initially communicate your pricing, regardless of how much confidence you exude when delivering it, and despite clarity in your proposal, your customers will ask for things. What is the most popular concession request a customer will make of you? *"We need a discount."*

We, as a business-to-business selling profession, have taught the buying community to ask for things. Purchasers of anything of substance know almost subconsciously the etymology of the word *propose*, which means "offer for consideration" or "suggest." A proposal is an *offered* plan.

I have been practicing, optimizing, studying, teaching, writing about, and speaking about the Four Levers for well over a decade. Yet every concession request we are about to go through still comes up periodically in my world. Organizations still ask. Practicing this framework, and specifically this concession request, will prepare you to handle any others that follow.

As discussed in chapter 1, the traditional approaches to handling the ask for a discount are often either (a) reminding the client of the "value" and the "return on investment," attempting to appeal to their logic; or (b) the ping-pong approach of firing off discounts in hopes that at some point the customer will say, "*That's good enough. We'll take it.*"

If you are trying to convince a buyer of your value when they're asking for a discount, that ship has long since sailed. Stop it.

If you give away discounts, you have simply become a charity, donating dollars to the customer's bottom line.

What's worse are the teachings of some that involve stretching the truth. For example, "*Well, this is going to be really difficult to get my CFO to agree to . . .*"–type language, when your CFO won't have anything to do with getting this done.

Without a framework, the discount giveaways are often softly paired with a fake expiration: "*We can give you 10% off if you can sign this week!*" In the customer's mind, you've now signaled a deadline from which the customer knows you will be increasingly desperate. And, without explaining why "this week" is important, the customer's mind has now filed the 10% discount into their brains for perpetuity and will most certainly take it regardless of whether they sign this week, next week, or next quarter.

This is where the Four Levers show their power.

STEP ONE: BE HUMAN

When a customer asks for a discount, we must listen intently and not be afraid to ask questions to clarify our understanding of the request's source. That is the simplicity of the "Be Human" step. We tend to want to solve the issue immediately, to throw up a bunch of logic to try to put out the fire. We must first understand the lens.

To start, let's think about the ways the customer asks for a discount:

1. *"We need to get the price down by $15,000, or we will have to focus our attention elsewhere."*

    Here, the customer is asking for a specific dollar amount discount. What questions do you have? My mind immediately wonders, *Why $15,000?* Is it a budget issue? Is it a perceived value issue?

2. *"We found an alternative that is 10% less than you. Match their price, and we're ready to move forward."*

    In this example, it sounds like they are indicating a desire to go with you as their vendor. Is this simply a request to help your customer sell internally and justify the purchase? Is there something else going on? Nothing is easier for a buyer than choosing between two products of the same price, but one is better than the other. Is that the goal of the customer here? *"So, if I'm hearing you correctly, you would prefer us, but we are priced a little higher?"*

3. *"Is there anything you can do to help us with the price?"*

    This may be someone who is looking for a helpful favor from you or someone with whom you have established a trusting relationship. This approach just recently came up in a conversation with one of my prospective clients. They asked, and I replied, "What are you looking for?" Simple. She replied, "Everyone is excited about bringing you in here, but it's just slightly higher than we were prepared to invest." Well, first of all, I should have set better expectations up front. But it is really good to know what is driving the request.

4. *"My spending limit is a few thousand dollars lower than your proposed price. Can we get this price down to $75,000? If we can't, I will have to involve others in the decision, which could slow this down and put the purchase at risk."*

Sounds like a very compelling reason to offer a discount, doesn't it? In many cases, different organizational levels have different budget access and spending authority. When you read these sentences above, what questions do you have? Ask them. Is this individual's spending limit $75,000? Is $75,000 all that's left in her budget? I would want to know what the process looks like once over $75,000.

However simple or compelling the ask, your approach to handling the ask should result in the same deal configurations for each customer.

To "Be Human" is simply conversing about the request so you can understand where it is coming from.

Be Human—The reason you are hired to sell goods is that you are a human being. Otherwise your employer would have sent a catalogue.

—Dr. Frank Crane, *Commandments of Salesmanship*, 1918

STEP TWO: REVIEW ALL FOUR LEVERS

Now we begin to address the question or concession request by reviewing the Four Levers. If we have laid the foundation properly, this won't be the first time they have heard the explanation of how the pricing is configured. Either way, reviewing the levers is necessary to serve as a foundation for the conversation and an agenda for addressing the request and establishing confidence that your price is your price.

To this point, as mentioned in chapter 6 when discussing the positioning of your price, while we have established that our price is what it is as of today, you may not have laid out the fourth lever yet, the Timing of the Deal: *"As you may recall from our conversations, our pricing is based on a set of core levers."*

1. Volume—or how much product/services you commit to.
2. Timing of Cash—or how fast you pay for the product/services.
3. Length of Commitment—or how long you commit to the product/services.

(If you have not talked about the fourth lever yet, you can introduce it here.)

4. Timing of the Deal—or mutual alignment around when you will be ready to sign and begin.

STEP THREE: DISCUSS USING ALL FOUR LEVERS

"Based on these Four Levers, maybe we can go through each and see if we can get you where you need to be."

In other words, use the Four Levers as the agenda for the discussion. All four of the levers! **Do not assume which lever they will want to pull. Do not pull levers for them. Do not propose.**

Instead, simply walk through each lever, one at a time, and discuss. The client is looking for a reduction in the spend on this purchase . . . so, start with the first lever.

1) Volume

If the client is willing to grow their commitment, the per-item price goes down, right? Think about the massive bottle of Hidden Valley Ranch dressing at your local warehouse shopping club. Because you are buying a larger amount, the per-ounce (or per-kilogram) amount you are paying goes down. Is this client anticipating growth? Can they accelerate that commitment now?

However, when you buy a giant tub of mayonnaise, the per-ounce or per-kilogram amount is lower but you just spent more than you would have if you bought a smaller jar at the local grocery store.

"Looking at Volume, the more products/services/technology you are committing to, the better and the more we are willing to pay you in the form of a discount.

"Understanding your desire to (reduce the price by $10,000 / lower the investment to below your approval threshold / etc.), this may only be valuable now if you anticipate future needs and want to lower the overall investment.

"However, understanding that the core driver of your price is Volume, to lower the dollar amount of the spend, it may end up meaning you will need to commit to less . . . although there are the other levers to look at first."

Then, pause . . . discuss. Might they want to grow the purchase? Buy the add-ons now? Include another division so they can combine budgets and benefit both? Listen, discuss, and then proceed to the second lever.

2) Timing of Cash

What are the payment terms you have proposed to the customer? Are they to pay monthly? Quarterly? What are the NET payment terms? NET30? NET45? Remember, you, the selling party, want to be paid faster rather than slower. There is value in quicker payments.

As discussed in chapter 3, we offered to pay the oil services company in the form of a discount to accelerate their out-year payments. They were making a three-year commitment, and they agreed to pay for Years 2 and 3 up front along with their Year 1 payment for a discount.

"The second lever is the Timing of Cash. The faster you are willing to pay for our products/technology/services, the better, and the more we are willing to pay you in the form of a discount.

"The proposal is based on you making monthly payments. If you are willing to pay us annually, up front, that's something we are willing to pay for in the form of a 5% discount."

Again, pause and listen. Let them discuss their flexibility in working with this second lever.

What happens if there is no place to go with this lever, meaning the customer is already committed to paying a single, up-front payment, NET30, and is only committing to a single year? Still, review this lever. Remind them.

"There's really not much we can do with this Timing of Cash lever, given that your pricing is already based on up-front, annual, NET30 payment terms, so let's look at the next one."

Do not skip a lever you believe can't be moved. When you skip a lever because you don't believe there is any room for the customer to adjust for it, the customer often adjusts it in the *opposite* direction. So, the reminder is there to proactively address when a customer says something like, "Oh, we can pay the higher amount if we can spread out the payments." Or: "We want to pay when the product is implemented, not when the contract is signed."

Faster payment = good.

Slower payment = bad.

3) Length of Commitment

What is the structure of the agreement in terms of how long they are required to commit to your products, technology, and/or services? Are they required to commit for a single year? A month at a time? Multiple years? Now is the time to walk the customer through the fact that a longer commitment to your solutions is worth paying for in the form of their desired concession, which, in this case, is a lessened dollar outlay.

"The third lever is the Length of Commitment. The longer you are willing to commit to our solutions, the better it is for us and our organization, and as such, is something we are willing to pay for in the form of a discount."

Make sure the customer is reminded that a core tenet of your pricing is based on the commitment as stated in the proposal, and then have a discussion on their ability to extend said commitment: "Your pricing today is based on an X-year commitment. For every additional year you are willing to commit to, we are willing to pay you in the form of a 5% discount."

4) The Timing of the Deal

Your organization cares greatly about forecast accuracy, doesn't it? Why do we fail to remind customers of this when discussing signature timing? Instead, we throw fake discounts around that expire at the end of the quarter. We somehow think the customer actually believes that your discount is a one-time, never-to-exist-again discount, and missing out on it will cause regret for the rest of their lives. Stop it.

Instead, remind the customer of the value of forecastability. Predicting when a customer will sign requires them to indicate when they will sign. Predicting when a customer will sign is not something you can necessarily motivate. And the value of an accurate forecast is worth paying for. It helps organizations make better decisions, enables better cash flow strategies, aligns resource investment and allocation with demand, helps with profitability, and ultimately results in higher customer satisfaction. Forecast accuracy also has a big impact on investor confidence, which leads to more investment.

Remember, it is best to save this fourth lever for later in the sales process. If a customer has not made a decision, does not know their own processes, and is early in their evaluation, *mutual* alignment around timing is impossible, so wait until it can be made with mutual confidence.

So, if you haven't shared an explanation of this fourth lever yet, now is the time.

"The fourth lever is the Timing of the Deal. There is tremendous value in our ability to predict our business. While you can probably guess we have targets to hit, more importantly, there's so much value in our organization's ability to predict when resources will be needed, etc. If you are willing to help us forecast, that mutual alignment around timing is something we are willing to pay for in the form of a discount."

Remember, your customer's organization cares about forecasting too. Every for-profit company finds value in predictability and can empathize with it. Why do we so often forget the *why* when explaining this?

A time-bound discount cannot be artificial. If you are dying to say, "Hey, we can give you a discount if you sign this week," I'd implore you to reconsider. You have just told the customer that a better price can be had. You have just reset the customer's expectation of what they will pay regardless of when they sign, as they will demand it.

A time-bound discount must be mutual and based on a customer's ability to execute and willingness to exchange dollars for the gem of predictability.

So, discuss their timing. Ask questions about what steps remain. How long should the process take? Is there a time frame you would feel comfortable aligning to? Are there steps your customer may not be considering? Be their sherpa!

Create a little buffer. Things happen. If a customer aligns with you around a specific date, add a couple of weeks for when *stuff happens*. Steps get injected. Fires within organizations happen. Knowing this is likely to happen is a core idea around *predicting*. If random delays always happen when aligning around timing, plan for it to happen again. In the story of the oil services company, the customer's original estimate was two to six weeks from the middle of July, which would have, in the worst case, had a signature coming at the beginning of September. We aligned around an end-of-September signature, accounting for the things we couldn't predict, which would inevitably slow down the process. And I'm so glad we did.

———

Simply put, when the customer asks for a discount, start by being a human. Ask them why. Next, remind them of how the pricing model is configured by reviewing all Four Levers. Finally, use each lever, one by one, to help the customer find their own discounts by either committing to more Volume, paying faster (Timing of Cash), extending the Length of their Commitment, or mutually aligning around the Timing of the Deal.

CHAPTER 10

Term and Termination Requests

**Every failure to maintain a price policy makes
the succeeding attempt more difficult.**
—*J. George Frederick, Modern
Salesmanagement, 1919*

F ollowing our meeting in Houston, the process of formalizing our
arrangement officially began. This transaction required a master
licensing agreement, which would cover the terms of the arrangement:
who will do what, when, and for how much.

After sending the agreement to the client, their lawyers reviewed it,
marking up different paragraphs, crossing out certain terms, and, in one
specific case, adding a paragraph.

The added paragraph? Termination for Convenience, which is a clause that allows the customer to terminate the contract at any time and for any reason. This clause removes the need to prove fault in order to terminate: No party has to have violated any terms of the agreement. It is simple language designed to give the customer the ultimate level of flexibility in case their desires or circumstances change.

Upon review of the client's markups and redlines, we immediately redlined out the Termination for Convenience paragraph, which removes any predictability to your contract. If a client has committed to a year or even a multiyear relationship with you, but this paragraph exists in your contract, it is as though there is no relationship at all. The customer can leave you the next day if they desire. In other words, having an out clause in a customer agreement is highly undesirable for you while highly desirable for the client.

As such, in the next round of reviews, they added the clause back in. We redlined it back out, and so on. Finally, with only a few contract elements left to review, we arranged a call between our lawyer and theirs. David and I were also on the call. Word edits and clarifications were the theme of the call until we reached the aforementioned term: Termination for Convenience.

What should you do?

When telling this story to a large technology company's sales organization, I asked that question. Immediately, my audience's COO raised his hand and shouted, "We tell them it's not our policy." He added that Termination for Convenience is a "nonstarter" and a "deal-breaker." I agree. It should be. Termination for Convenience should never exist in any of your customer contracts. However, "it's not our policy" is not how to communicate it to the customer.

I replied, "With all due respect, the customer doesn't give a crap about your policy." Probably not the best way to respond to a C-level executive in front of his entire team.

"It's not our policy" and "it's a nonstarter" are fighting words for a customer. The customer's policy is "it IS our policy to have that language included in a contract," and "it's potentially a deal-breaker." Suddenly, all the trust you've built is gone. Instead of having a mutual understanding based on trust, you have put yourselves in an adversarial position. There's a better way to have a conversation that builds trust and mutual understanding.

HOW TO RESPOND

Use the response framework discussed in the previous chapter: "Be Human," "Review All Four Levers," and "Discuss Using All Four Levers."

Step One: Be Human

Being human means simply having a conversation about what is driving the request. In this interaction, upon getting to this portion of the agreement, this means simply clarifying the "why."

I asked, "We are now to the Termination for Convenience language you requested. As you have noticed, we had redlined this out, but it appears as though it is important to you. Can you tell us a little about why? Why have you added that clause to our agreement?"

They responded by sharing two primary reasons: "First, Termination for Convenience is a clause we require to be in every one of our vendor contracts. Second, the oil services industry is highly unpredictable. It is very difficult for us to be able to predict what direction the industry will go year-to-year and how that will impact our allocation of resources. So, we need the flexibility to be able to exit the contract when necessary."

So, now the customer has had a chance to share why this language is important to them; it is (supposedly) a company policy, and they need the flexibility this language provides. Got it.

Step Two: Review All Four Levers

By reviewing all Four Levers, you are doing three things:

1. You are giving yourself a chance to think.
2. You are reinforcing the makeup of the entire agreement, not just a single portion.
3. You are reinforcing the sound basis by which your pricing is made up.

"As you may recall, the agreement and associated pricing are based on four core levers. The first is Volume, or how much you are purchasing. The second is the Timing of Cash, which reflects our agreement around paying for the entire term up front. The third is the Length of Commitment, where your price is based on a three-year commitment. The fourth is the Timing of the Deal. We have mutually aligned around you helping us with our forecast by committing to sign in September, which is also reflected in your price."

That's it. You have reminded them of the levers. Now, it's time to address the specific issue.

Step Three: Discuss Using All Four Levers

While, in this example, it should be clear what lever we will be talking about the most, do not make the assumption for them as to which lever is best to pull. You will see this more emphatically in how we address upcoming concession requests. However, here's how to proceed in the discussion in this example.

"Specific to Termination for Convenience, you can have it, but you are probably not going to like it. Termination for Convenience represents no Length of Commitment. As such, your pricing would have to change . . . pretty dramatically. Your price is based on a three-year commitment to our technology and services. A contract with Termination for Convenience would require us to price this based on our month-to-month pricing, which is at least 30 to 35% higher. I can have David provide that estimate."

I then added, "Remember, there are protections in this agreement under Warranties and Termination for Cause. If our solutions don't do what we have represented them to do, you have remedies, including the ability to terminate the agreement. However, if our solutions do what we represent them to do, the pricing is commensurate with the Length of Commitment. While we have each of our lawyers on the call here together, should we take a look at the Warranty language and Termination for Cause language to ensure those cover most instances where you would desire to terminate?"

Given we were on a conference call, unable to see one another, the phone went very quiet. I imagine that the customer was not quite sure what to do with my response. Or, as professional negotiators themselves, maybe they were using the silent treatment as a psychological tactic. When silence goes unacknowledged, it is highly uncomfortable for our brains. In many cases, the pressure of extended silence without explanation forces us to want to fill the silence. That desire can then cause a less-than-confident salesperson to try to immediately *solve* the issue for the customer.

Given that David and I were also in different locations, we communicated with each other on a direct messaging app. I DM'd David, "Let them be the next ones to speak. Put your phone on mute if you have to."

After a brief moment (which felt, to us, like 30 seconds), Fred spoke up. "David, yes, we should take a look at what the pricing would be with the commitment removed. And yes, let's take a look at that existing clause language to make sure it covers what we need."

Sure enough, the Termination for Convenience request disappeared. We made some minor modifications to the Termination for Cause language together. They understood, assessed whether the flexibility of a

Termination for Convenience clause was ultimately worth the added expense, and realized quickly that it was not.

In hindsight, I believe they asked because they could. Why not ask for the commitment to be removed? Without the Four Levers framework, we may have immediately given in, started a battle, or revealed a crack in our foundation. The conversation was easy, and they never even followed up asking for the month-to-month pricing.

WHAT HAPPENS WHEN THE CUSTOMER "WINS" TERMINATION FOR CONVENIENCE?

As a growing company going upmarket to larger companies and larger opportunities, we had a big fish on the hook. One of our enterprise-level salespeople received verbal communication that we had been selected to be the software provider for a significant consumer packaged goods (CPG) company generating over $5 billion in annual revenue. Our technology would be deployed across all of their brands, making it the largest deal in our company's history by a wide margin.

The negotiation progressed to where we were dealing with an individual in their procurement department. We'll call her Marianne because that was her name. Things had now intensified, and my CEO asked me to handle the conversations and final negotiation.

Marianne asked for the moon, and using the Four Levers, we quickly agreed on all of the commercial terms except for one: Termination for Convenience.

Using the structure discussed above, but in dealing with an individual who was not a part of any of the discussions leading up to this negotiation, we reached a quick understanding of each other's needs. She was asking for, actually demanding, Termination for Convenience in the agreement.

Her response to my question about why this was such an important element of the agreement was, "Every one of our vendor agreements has

Termination for Convenience language included, and it will be in this one too." She made it a bit difficult to have much more of a *human* conversation, so I went into Step Two, reviewing the levers, and Step Three, discussing the request using all Four Levers.

I explained to her that our pricing, as we had discussed, was based on four primary elements: how much they are buying, how fast they are paying, how long they are committing, and the mutual alignment around when they planned to sign. I explained, "A core tenet of the pricing we are finalizing is based on the commitment to our products, technology, and services. Termination for Convenience represents no commitment, so, fundamentally, the pricing and terms of the agreement would need to change to reflect that lack of commitment."

Her reply? "Todd, we must have Termination for Convenience. We are not willing to pay for it. Termination for Cause language does not address our need for flexibility. Either we have the language in the agreement, or we do not have an agreement."

The Length of Commitment was an even more important element of this agreement than just revenue predictability. This CPG company sold a wide range of products, collected reviews for those products, and, in some cases, the products being sold were of the OTC (over-the-counter) medication variety. Products with a medication classification require extra attention. If a consumer were to leave a product review mentioning a potential adverse effect from using the product, it had to be flagged and reported per government regulations. For our organization to handle medical product reviews, flagging, and reporting, we had to invest in specific resources. We hired a pharmacist to manually review the reviews. We built reporting workflows that required additional development and support. I explained this to her, but she didn't seem to empathize. She was a professional negotiator taking a hard stance. The Four Levers had disarmed much of the discussion regarding her concession requests, but not this one.

We left the conversation without an agreement. She was waiting me out, hoping to crack our confidence so that we would simply give in out of a desperate desire for their business.

Two days later, I had my regular weekly one-on-one with my CEO. The first question he asked? "Where is this deal?"

I replied, "Well, we're down to only one term in the agreement: Termination for Convenience. But you know me, I'm handling it."

My CEO replied, "Todd, that is the update you gave me days ago. This deal is incredibly important to the business. We have to get this done, and done immediately. The longer this goes on, the lower the odds are that it will happen at all. We are ending this discussion right now. Return to your office, call Marianne, and tell her we will accept the Termination for Convenience clause in exchange for an immediate signature."

Until then, my success in negotiating Termination for Convenience requests out of agreements was a perfect 100%. This one hurt. I walked back to my office like Charlie Brown from the *Peanuts* cartoons walking up his driveway after just checking his empty mailbox on Valentine's Day. I did what he asked. The agreement was signed soon after the discussion, with that paragraph included right in the heart of the agreement.

A few months later, my CEO, COO (chief operating officer), and I had completed a private equity "roadshow." We were attempting to raise a round of funding for our business, raising capital to continue investing and growing the company. We had completed sixteen pitches, received three offers with company valuations based on our stated current and expected revenues, and selected one that fit our current investors' expectations for this round.

When a private equity partner is selected, they send in forensic accountants to your office. These accountants are experts at reviewing your finances and reading your contracts to make sure their investment is based on accurate information and assumptions. Can you guess which agreement they read first? Yes, of course, the largest one. They went right to the agreement that represented a significant percentage of our revenues. They went right to the marquee account's contract that emblazoned our marketing efforts.

While sitting in our conference room, the accountant walked in, holding the agreement.

"Hey, in reading this agreement from (CPG Company), I noticed this paragraph."

He was pointing at the paragraph that had appeared in my nightmares for the months since that dreaded conversation with Marianne, the procurement beast.

After our attempts to explain how this paragraph "only appears in this agreement" and how we "would not have been able to secure the agreement without agreeing to that term," we quickly learned that this private equity firm viewed this *multiyear* agreement as a monthly agreement, regardless of how long it might take for a company of this customer's size to remove our solution and replace it with another. We learned that our valuation would affect their investment in us.

Every investor understands Termination for Cause language. Warranty provisions are understandable too. But if your solutions don't deliver as promised, your problems go far beyond the words in an agreement. However, the word *convenience* nullifies commitment. Convenience is completely out of your control. Your value does not matter. Your execution does not matter. Your impact does not matter. The client can wake up one day and simply decide, *"Meh, we don't need this."* A company cannot predict without commitments, which means an investor absolutely cannot predict without commitments.

THE OUT CLAUSE PENALTY OPTION

In selling to a direct-selling company in the beauty care space, I, along with three others in our organization, flew to New York to present to their buying team. Following a great discussion, we offered to take them out to dinner, and they accepted. A couple of the project sponsors, team members, and the buying agent named Jeff from the client came out with us. We ate. We had a couple of drinks. We became fast friends.

Once back at our offices, we sent over the agreement, and the negotiation began. We settled on a one-year commitment to their needed Volume of our solutions for $110,000. The Timing of Cash was agreed upon to be paid up front with NET30 payment terms. Everything looked great.

Sure enough, along with some minor requests and word changes to the agreement itself, Jeff (the buying agent) added the dreaded paragraph into our agreement: Termination for Convenience.

As part of the back-and-forth with the agreement over email, we redlined the Termination for Convenience clause out of the agreement. They added it back in. It was time for the discussion. This time, it was just a phone call between me and Jeff.

While engaging in Step One: Be Human, I asked him why he requested that paragraph. He explained that the company had been facing some financial issues, which were known to the public, so this was no surprise. He added that he "needed this paragraph" in the agreement.

I then reminded him of how the pricing had been configured, reviewing Step Two with him—a review of all Four Levers. Then, on to Step Three, I explained how Termination for Convenience represents no commitment, how it's a core tenet to the pricing, and that something else (aka, either the price itself or the remaining three levers beyond Length of Commitment) would have to be adjusted to reflect the elimination of any commitment.

He replied, "Todd, I understand. We are not in a position to pay for it. I just need this paragraph to be in the agreement."

I was curious. He had said how he, himself, *needed* this paragraph in the agreement. Since our discussions had extended beyond just business-to-business interactions, I took the Be Human step to another level.

"Jeff, I'm not sure where to go here. Our price is our price based on the levers that drive it. You've mentioned how you need this. Why is this so important to you?"

He replied, "Todd, it's probably bad form that I'm sharing this, but part of how I am measured in this role is based on the percentage of agreements where the language of Termination for Convenience appears."

This was different. Jeff was telling me how important these three words, Termination for Convenience, were to his pay and how his performance was measured. I replied with an idea. It was a Hail Mary that would help both organizations.

"What if we agreed to include Termination for Convenience language in the agreement; however, if you and your organization decided to leverage that language and terminate for convenience, you would still owe us the full $110,000?"

After some quick discussion about this idea, Jeff agreed. We would include the Termination for Convenience, but the predictable revenue from the agreement would not change a single dollar, whether they used this language or not.

When you take a step back and think about it, this is a ridiculous idea. We have given this language no teeth by associating a penalty for using the term equal to the amount they would spend if they did not use it.

Jeff accepted.

Our ability to accept this language did not impact our expected revenue, so it was acceptable. However, I do not recommend taking this approach unless absolutely necessary.

The lesson? Termination for Convenience negatively impacts your organization's ability to predict revenue, which in turn impacts its ability to confidently make investments to support anticipated growth. This is also why those who invest in your organization will do so without hesitancy, feeling confident that as long as your organization continues to deliver on its promises, revenue can be predicted.

CHAPTER 11

"Will You Hold the Price?"

You have often created an adverse impression
by an air of hesitancy and apology. If you are
afflicted with this failing, you must overcome
it. Confidence is begotten of honest intention,
consciousness of ability and conviction of
the worth of the thing we have to sell.
—Forbes-Lindsay, The Psychology of a Sale, 1914

Eight weeks had passed since our in-person negotiation had taken place in Houston. The discussion began with a request for a significant discount. Through that discussion, we had uncovered the driver of the request, walked them through the Four Levers, and settled on an agreement.

We would be paying them in the form of a discount in exchange for the acceleration of payment—the Timing of Cash. Instead of paying each of the three years of the agreement at the beginning of each year, they would pay the entire amount up front.

We also would be paying them in the form of a discount to help us forecast—the Timing of the Deal. We had mutually aligned around the timing of when they would be prepared to sign. There was a mutual understanding of the value of predictable timing on our business and how their help was worth providing them with a 5% discount.

Regarding the Timing of the Deal, they had skin in the game. While we could have attempted to accelerate their purchase, the power of the Timing of the Deal lever is in the collaboration in determining the *when*. While eight weeks had passed, they had initially estimated a typical two- to six-week time frame from where we were in July. We had given them a buffer and were paying them to help us forecast this transaction for a September close.

Sure enough, David's phone rang on September 23. It was Fred from the oil services company.

"David! Hey, I have a question for you. We had no way of knowing this was going to be an issue. However, as we're routing this agreement for final signature, it turns out the final signer is on vacation through next week [aka, the end of September]. He will be back on Monday, October 1. Can you confirm that you can hold the agreed-upon price until next month?"

What do you do? The answer, as with every concession request, is to stay true to the Four Levers.

STEP ONE: BE HUMAN

Show that you have listened. Fred had indicated that the individual who would be the signer was on vacation. Who is it? Where did he go on vacation?

"Oh, he's on a submarine at the bottom of the Atlantic Ocean and won't have access to the internet?"

"Oh, he's on a spaceship to visit Mars and has no access to Docusign?"

I say those things in jest, but having a nonconfrontational beginning to the conversation is helpful. And, in this case, you are clarifying whether this person is completely "off the grid" on vacation. You are clarifying who this person is and whether anyone else is taking responsibility while they are away. You are being a human being.

STEP TWO: REVIEW ALL FOUR LEVERS

"Okay. Well, as you recall, your pricing is based on the Four Levers we have been discussing. How much you buy [Volume]. How fast you pay [Timing of Cash]. How long you are committing [Length of Commitment]. And our mutual alignment around the timing of the signature [Timing of the Deal]. The price has been established based on mutual alignment around the timing, from which we are paying you that value in our ability to forecast, in the form of a 5% discount."

It is a simple review and reminder of the pricing model—one paragraph, a few sentences. With this reminder, begin to address the request to hold your price beyond the mutually agreed-upon timing.

STEP THREE: DISCUSS USING ALL FOUR LEVERS

Now, when addressing the request, start with three simple words (if, of course, you count a contraction as one word):

"I don't know."

Yes. A simple "I don't know." You will add a little more context below, but those simple words are intended to add *uncertainty* to the request.

Uncertainty can make our brains go a little crazy. We are all wired to anticipate. We are prediction machines. Uncertainty makes us uneasy and drives us to attempt to quell that uneasiness by creating certainty for ourselves.[5]

If you need any proof that uncertainty creates certainty-seeking behavior, sometimes to a crazy level, remember back to March 2020. The world was shutting down due to the COVID pandemic. We were all told to stay home for a period of time. "Shelter in place" was the prevailing guidance. There was no way to know for how long.

Consumer goods manufacturers were not prepared for what was to come. Supply was designed to meet the demands of the regular consumers, who purchase what they need for the week or maybe even two weeks. However, the buzz that two weeks could turn longer created uncertainty, which created a hoarding mentality. Specifically, the first item everyone wanted to ensure they had in perpetuity was toilet paper. Individuals ran to the grocery shelves and bought up every roll in sight. Shelves of two-ply were barren for weeks. (Funnily enough, if you looked hard enough, there were still a few rolls of one-ply around, but who wants that?)

When asked if you will hold the price until next month, the goal is to create honest uncertainty around the request.

We tend to want to create certainty ourselves. We prefer not to cause uneasiness for our customers. That's commendable. But the truth should be that you have created a forecast based on their *mutual* alignment. The truth should be that your company is planning on this transaction being signed based on that mutual alignment, which allows the organization to solve for the uneasiness of investors, invest, and prepare resources to ensure readiness to help your customer achieve their desired outcomes with your solutions.

So, your answer should start with, "*I don't know.*" You can add, "*As mentioned, your pricing is based on us paying for predictability. There was and is still value in that predictability, which we are paying you for in the form of your price. Let's talk about October when October gets here. What I do know for sure is if we can find a way to get this signed, still here in September, that price remains."*

Then, be quiet. Let them respond.

The minute you create certainty, the minute destiny is assured.

If you were, instead, to respond with, "*No! That price goes away at midnight on September 30. We had an agreement,*" trust erodes. Your customer becomes considerably more upset than with an "I don't know" answer. To the customer, they can't fathom why a signature a few hours later, aka the next morning of October 1, would create so much consternation.

And, what's worse, if the price does go up 5% on October 1, they may need to start over. It is likely they have already allocated the budget. In this example, Fred shared that your deal is at the end of the approval process. A new price might cause the approval process to start over completely, risking further elongation of the process. Instead of a late September deal, your deal may slide to the end of October, the end of November, or maybe never.

If you were, instead, to respond with, "*Sure. As long as it is signed first thing in the morning on October 1, I will make sure the pricing stays in place,*" your deal would have just slid to October. And, what's worse, you have paid for something—end-of-September predictability—and didn't receive it.

By responding with, "I don't know. Let's talk about next month next month," you have stayed true to your pricing. You have created a slight level of uneasiness in the buyer's brain, which will drive them further to either pursue a firm answer or figure out a way to get your contract signed in the absence of the final approver.

In this case, Fred replied to David's "I don't know," with, "Well, we kind of need to know. If the price goes up, we may have to revisit budget approvals and start the process over."

David's response: "I understand. Unfortunately, we can't know the answer until we see how our month ends."

Fred didn't love the conversation, understandably, but the alternatives are either an erosion of trust, an elongated deal cycle, or us paying for something we will not receive.

Fred called me next. "Todd, I just got off the phone with David. Here's the situation . . ."

Fred explained, much like he had with David, his challenge in getting this signed per our mutual agreement. However, this time, he shared an understanding of "I know you are paying us to get this done this month."

My answer was the same as David's. "I understand. However, I don't know. We can revisit this first thing in the morning on October 1 if you cannot secure a signature."

Sure enough, in this instance, Fred's organization sent a Docusign link to the eSignature signer, who was not *completely* away, and the transaction was signed.

They wired us the entire dollar amount just before Halloween.

When the Client Is Late

Now, what would have happened if they had not signed on time? Using the Four Levers to ensure Timing of the Deal aids forecasting accuracy in a big way, but it is not completely foolproof.

Imagine it is October 1. The contract is not signed. David talks to Fred, who asks again, "David, I can run this over to our CFO right now for signature. Is the price still the price?"

Now it's a judgment call for you and your organization. In many cases, we would still take the deal as negotiated, even though we were not receiving what we were paying for.

"Fred, although we aren't quite getting what we paid for"—said with a smile—"there's still value in completing this transaction right now." As a privately held organization, the difference may be negligible. Your resources have to wait only one more day to be deployed to a new project. And, remembering my days when I would have to present to a board of directors a few weeks later, there was value in telling the investors, "*Yes, we missed the quarter due to a deal slipping, but it was signed the next day.*"

This decision is up to you and your leadership team. If you have a trusting relationship with the client and there is value in taking the transaction off the table and not prolonging it, take it. But explain the *why*. Without it, when the customer seeks to buy more from you, the Timing of the Deal lever will lose significance. As a matter of fact, future deal timing alignment is strengthened through that explanation.

On the other hand, sometimes your client is habitually unreliable. They have missed forecast alignment around the Timing of the Deal multiple times. In those cases, it may be a good idea to communicate to the customer, "*Unfortunately, as you recall, one important element of your pricing was our mutual alignment around the timing. We were paying you in the form of a discount to help us forecast our business, and that didn't happen. Let's take a fresh look at this pricing. Maybe there are other ways for us to pay you that 5%.*"

Then, explore the other three levers with them again. Maybe they can lengthen their commitment. Maybe they can add some products or services. Maybe they can pay you a little faster.

Either way, you have created a *sound basis* that builds trust and integrity in your pricing model and avoids a discounting pandemic that is sure to follow for future transactions.

Keep in mind *mutual alignment* is required for this to be effective. The "I don't know" approach to handling requests regarding whether your Timing of the Deal incentive can be extended only works when you have had mutual alignment earlier in the process. Without it, without the customer's firm understanding of the *why* around that incentive and them having skin in the game, you run the risk of sounding like every other salesperson slinging fake expiring discounts.

CHAPTER 12

Payment Term Needs

*Once upon a time there was a bear who was
hungry and a man who was cold, so they
decided to negotiate in a neutral cave. After
several hours a settlement was reached.
When they emerged the man had a fur coat
and the bear was no longer hungry.*
—Chester L. Karrass, The Negotiating Game, 1969

"WE WOULD LIKE TO PAY MONTHLY INSTEAD OF MAKING A SINGLE, UP-FRONT ANNUAL PAYMENT"

"Todd, can you help me with something? I'm trying to finalize the agreement with Anika over at Avery & Co. She's upset at one of the terms in our proposal. Can you speak with her?" asked Dante, my always confident salesperson who had just gotten bull-rushed during a negotiation.

"Sure," I replied. Dante and I discussed the situation, and within a few minutes, Anika and I were having a conversation.

Anika was the digital marketing manager for a company specializing in higher-end women's clothing, fragrances, and jewelry. She had demanded Dante connect her with his "manager."

Anika exclaimed, "Todd, you and your entire company are totally out of touch with the digital marketing industry. Every email marketing solution on the market offers monthly billing. But here comes—la-di-da—your company, forcing me to pay up front for the entire year!"

I could hear the frustration in her voice. This was her way of saying, "*We need to pay monthly.*" She was representing her organization, her department, and her budget, and the idea of changing from a current vendor who bills them smaller amounts 12 times per year to one, larger invoice was clearly a big issue.

Step One: Be Human

After hearing her out, I attempted to be human. I repeated back to her what I believed the question to be: "Okay. I understand. And you're right. Our proposal is based on an annual, up-front payment. Monthly billing sounds really important for you. Is that a process issue? Budget? Cash flow?"

She snapped back, "Our processes are set up for monthly billing."

Step Two: Review All Four Levers

"Anika, we have built our pricing model around four foundational levers. Your pricing is based on how much Volume you are committing to, how fast you pay [Timing of Cash], how long you commit [Length of Commitment], and we have mutually aligned around your timing [Timing of the Deal]."

Step Three: Discuss Using All Four Levers

"The price you have before you is based on an up-front, annual payment, due NET30. If you'd like to pay monthly, you can, but we would need to adjust one of the other elements to address this change."

———

The vibe completely changed . . . instantly. The price is the price. The levers provide the flexibility. If the customer wants to pay a little slower, they can either pay a little more, buy a little more, commit a little longer, or align around timing. Today, many pricing pages for services on websites reflect the difference between paying monthly and paying annually. It is a common practice. This conversation happened in 2011.

We understood each other. She wanted to talk through what would have to change to adjust for monthly billing, but before getting into the details, I asked her one more question: "Do you know if your organization really enjoys paying monthly? We base our pricing on annual payments because, frankly, it's less work. There is less tracking down of payments and purchase orders. Less processing time. But, the funny thing is, many of our clients prefer to pay annually, too, for exactly the same reason."

"It's a good question." She didn't have an answer. Anika was a leader in Avery's marketing department. The core of her desire to pay monthly was simply from a "this is how we have always done it" perspective.

I piled on. "I am also guessing that, when you sign an agreement like this, you allocate its amount from your annual budget, not a month at a time. In other words, when you sign this agreement, your finance team will carve out $57,600 immediately, not $4,800 monthly." The conversation finished with her commitment to check with her finance team about whether they would prefer to pay annually.

The agreement was signed the following day with one up-front annual payment.

Curious, I asked Dante if he had spoken to Anika about the conversation she had with finance. He hadn't but was scheduled to speak with her about scheduling the kickoff.

"Can you ask her for me?" I asked. He did.

"She said they actually don't care whether payment happens annually or monthly. The amount of this contract makes up a small percentage of their marketing budget anyway, so taking advantage of annual versus monthly pricing makes sense."

However, she also told Dante something else interesting, which I'm guessing many may believe to be a good reason to pay monthly. Dante said, "She also said that, with new contracts, finance prefers to pay monthly just in case the solution isn't delivering as promised. They prefer to have not paid yet versus trying to use Termination for Cause or Warranty provisions in the contract to get a refund."

If you are thinking, *Hmmm, that's a good reason!* I'd suggest thinking about it this way: If our solutions were not functioning as promised, we would be in breach of the agreement. That is exactly why terms like Termination for Cause and Warranty provisions exist to remedy those situations. When a customer, instead of leveraging those contract terms, decides to withhold payment, they are now also breaching. Remedying a contract breach by also breaching the contract is not recommended.

Beginning in 2011, I joined ExactTarget. By early 2013, most of the organization, including our partners, was leveraging Four Levers conversations. In 2013, we were acquired by the American cloud-based software company Salesforce.com for $2.5B in cash.[6]

One of the first adjustments we were asked to make was to drive a considerably higher percentage of our customers to annual billing. It was a mandate from Salesforce's founder and CEO, Marc Benioff, who, at the time, told our leadership team, "Any contract, new or renewal, that has anything other than annual billing terms must be approved by me." It did not matter whether it was a $5,000 or $5,000,000 account. He wanted eyes on every single one of the contracts where monthly or quarterly billing existed.

It was a terrifying thought, asking Marc for payment term approval for even the smallest deals. I didn't want to think about it, and neither did our leadership team. So, I was asked to help double down on the Four Levers. The combination of "stick" via Benioff's approval requirement plus additional "carrot" training didn't take long to make a considerable impact, where we had raised our annually billed clients dramatically.

Why did Marc care so much?

While reducing the level of effort required to collect from customers can result in efficiencies, the investment community views a high amount of deferred revenue on a balance sheet favorably.

Deferred revenue, also known as unearned revenue, refers to advance payments a company receives for products or services that are to be delivered or performed in the future. The company that receives the prepayment records the amount as deferred revenue, a liability on its balance sheet.[7]

Put simply, collecting cash faster equals higher "deferred revenue," which is a sign of strong cash flow and financial stability. It generates predictability and visibility from the investment community. Higher deferred revenue indicates predictability for investors and stable growth of expected revenue.

It is also a sign of customer retention. Higher amounts of deferred revenue give investors more confidence in your solutions, as it typically reflects a longer commitment.

As you continue to use and grow in the Four Levers, you'll find that many of the requests you receive from customers are being asked for without the customers truly understanding why they are asking for them. Even in my own business today, my customers often ask to pay slowly. When an answer is given with confidence through the levers, the requests just disappear.

Remember, while your organization desires faster payments, and the companies you are selling to thrive on faster payments, individual buyers and buying organizations prefer the opposite. They will ask. You must set the lever.

When a client asks for monthly billing, ask why. Review the pricing model based on the Four Levers. Then discuss the impact of monthly billing and the flexibility provided by the levers moving up or down.

TRADING LEVER FOR LEVER

Your levers do not always have to have a dollar cost associated with them.

Monthly billing is a request to pay slowly. Your pricing is based on the customer paying more rapidly—aka annually. When reviewing the levers with the customer, it does not necessarily mean you should tell them, *"Oh, you want to pay monthly? Well, our pricing is based on paying annually. You're gonna have to pay for it!"*

While organizations are now used to the idea that paying monthly will cost more than paying annually, and you can communicate that, remember that the levers are there to allow the customer to *pay for* slower payment terms in other ways.

Would you and your organization be willing to allow the customer to pay quarterly or monthly (versus annually) in exchange for committing to additional Volume? *"Buy more stuff, and we'll pay you for that in the form of slower payment terms."*

How about in exchange for adding to their Length of Commitment? If a customer is willing to add years to their commitment, is it worth you allowing them to pay more slowly over that period?

How about in exchange for predictability through the Timing of the Deal? If a customer is willing to help you forecast, is that worth them paying a little more slowly?

These are all up to you and your organization. The point is, while each lever has a cost associated with it, a customer asking to push a lever in one direction should not automatically mean you throw dollars on top in exchange. Instead, think of pulling the other levers in balance.

"OUR STANDARD PAYMENT TERMS ARE NET60"

Your customers would prefer to hold on to their money as long as possible. You probably feel the same way. *"Buy now, pay later"* is the marketing cry of many an organization, dating all the way back to the 1800s. If it costs you nothing to pay later, why wouldn't you? The pay-later mindset is inherent to us as human beings.

Most organizations offer customers NET30 payment terms. In other words, *"Here is your invoice. You have a month to pay."*

When you go to a grocery store, clothing store, or gas station, your payment terms are "pay on receipt." You are required to pay for the items before you leave with them. Having a month to pay for the items you are likely providing sounds like a good deal, right? Well, not for finance teams. Having more cash on hand is always of value to finance, regardless of how big or small the purchase.

You've proposed the deal to your customer: *"$100,000, to be paid up front annually, NET30, based on a one-year commitment."* Often, the last concession request you will hear is, *"Our standard payment terms are NET60,"* or something similarly longer than what you have proposed. It is as though the organization you are selling to is trying to sneak in the term. *"Hey, we're just gonna pay you a month later. It's our policy."*

Should you reply like Chris Farley from the 1995 classic sales movie *Tommy Boy* and simply say, "Okey dokey!"? Would your local grocery store be okay if you were to sneak in a payment term: *"My standard is NET14. I'll pay you for these apples in two weeks"*? In many organizations, the common answer from salespeople is equivalent to responding, *"We can't do NET14 on your shopping cart, but we can do NET7. Would that work? A week to pay?"* It's silly if you think about it.

Step One: Be Human

Depending on how this concession request is framed, you likely do not need to delve too deeply into the ask. It's often safe to assume that the NET60 request is simply based on a desire to hold on to their money for another month. However, if the customer were to say, *"We need the pricing term to be NET60,"* the simple response would be, *"Why?"*

Why else would a customer be asking for more time to pay your invoice? Maybe the agreement is being signed during one fiscal period, but they need to wait until the next fiscal period to outlay the payment. Maybe the company is going through some sort of funding event. Maybe the company is going through an audit. There could be many reasons why they ask to pay slowly. These answers, while they do not impact the delivery of your response, could impact how you contract out years in an agreement.

Step Two: Review All Four Levers

Yes, I know it may sound almost nauseating to keep saying "the Four Levers" over and over again to the client, but do it. You are delivering the sound basis of your pricing to the customer. They are being reminded that the price is the price, and the terms are the terms, and when one term moves, another needs to move in an opposite direction. The levers are being reinforced to the point where the customer will remember them come renewal time, when they want to purchase more from you, or when they look to make a purchase from you in their next position or company.

Step Three: Discuss Using All Four Levers

"Regarding the Timing of Cash, your pricing is based on NET30 payment terms. If you need to move that to NET60 you can, but something else will need to be changed to reflect that adjustment."

Then, using ALL of the levers, having discussed one of them already, which is the Timing of Cash, discuss what you are willing to pay for in the form of longer payment terms.

Would you be willing to allow the customer to pay more slowly in exchange for a larger commitment to Volume? Maybe.

Would you be willing to allow the customer to pay more slowly in exchange for a longer Length of Commitment? Committing to extra years in exchange for extended payment terms? Probably.

Would you be willing to allow the customer to pay more slowly in exchange for accelerating the Timing of the Deal? Likely. However, be careful with this one. Unless the timing is *mutually* agreed upon, framed through the lens of assisting your organization's ability to forecast revenue, cash flow, and resource needs, artificially accelerating signatures is typically not a great idea.

For the customers I have taught this framework to, for my own sales organizations, and for my current business, oftentimes this request just goes away as a result of the three-step response discussed above.

As I was first building up my training and speaking organization a few years ago, I was negotiating a significant training engagement with one of the top-10 largest software companies in the world. I am obviously small potatoes compared to this logo. I was excited about finalizing this agreement as it would put a stamp on the sustainability of my business. *"I have product-market fit. Large companies are loving what I deliver, substantiated by the commitment they are about to make!"*

The client sent me the signed agreement initiated on their end via Docusign. However, the client changed the payment terms from NET30 to NET90 as they were signing the agreement. You read that correctly. NET90. Instead of having one month to pay my invoice, they gave themselves an undiscussed concession: the ability to take three months to pay. It was a next-level sneak maneuver. *"Todd, we adjusted the payment terms on this to our company standard."* Oh, did you? I assumed I was not the first who had experienced this approach, whereas I also assumed the customer gets away with it through the lens of, *"They'll be happy they have a signed agreement."* NET90 would create additional stress on my business. I would, as a solopreneur, be building out programs and delivering programs, yet would not see a dime for an entire quarter of the year.

It may feel insignificant to you as a salesperson to get a meaty deal signed and the organization has to wait a little longer to get paid. Maybe it doesn't even impact your commissions or goal achievement. However, it does matter to your organization. Imagine if word got out to your customer community that your customers can pay whenever they want; cash flow could quickly become a problem. Your existing and future customers would all come to expect extended payment flexibility. Renewal discussions could also turn into a perception of favoritism for some customers. While that may sound dramatic, human beings are dramatic! If, instead, you can trade their concession request for something you DO get paid for, wouldn't it be worth the conversation?

My response used the Four Levers. I started by asking about NET90, asking with a smile and a laugh, given I had never seen that payment term in the technology space before. I then explained to the sponsor and signer through Step Two how my pricing and business models work. Finally, I explained through Step Three, "My business is built on aligning payment to time of delivery. It is an important tenet of the price you have before you. If you want NET90, you can have it, but we will have to adjust something else to make up for it."

They immediately responded by countering with, "We can accept NET45." Is that a win? Not really, as, again, the pricing is based on NET30 payment terms, payment aligned to program delivery. I expressed my appreciation for their understanding but reminded them again through the Four Levers. (I also made a bit of a joke, which required me to have established a good relationship ahead of time: "In reality, the size of this agreement to you can probably be paid by the coins you find in the couch cushions of your lobby.")

Given that this was a short-term agreement, we settled on a trade for the Timing of the Deal. They signed the agreement immediately, two weeks earlier than originally anticipated, telling me to "invoice us this afternoon."

They received NET45 payment terms on the agreement, but I was able to invoice them two weeks earlier than originally planned, so, in the end, I was still getting paid at the exact same time I would have with NET30 payment terms.

Extended payment terms may seem like an insignificant concession; however, even the smallest concession can erode the sound basis of your pricing model in the eyes of your customers. Your business model relies on customer commitments and timely payments. Your confidence in that fact begets your customers' confidence and trust in you.

CHAPTER 13

Starting Smaller & Proof-of-Concept Requests

*Simple genuineness, transparency of character,
will win the confidence of a customer whether
he is prejudiced or not, and the confidence
of the purchaser is half the sale.*
—*Orison Swett Marden, Selling Things, 1916*

"WE NEED TO [LAST MINUTE] REDUCE OUR VOLUME COMMITMENT"

It was the final days of a significant deal. Every element of the agreement had been settled. It was down to the final signatures before one of my account executives, Eric, would punch his ticket for President's Club.

The customer was a direct-selling company that sells bags, totes, and other accessories through thousands of independent consultants. These consultants schedule small get-togethers in their communities to social-ize and sip a little vino, during which the bags are displayed, discussed, and sold to partygoers.

The deal was to initially arm 35,000 (Volume) of their almost 80,000 consultants with marketing technology that would allow them to pro-mote the get-togethers, confirm attendees, send reminders, and handle transaction notifications and receipts. The client would be paying a sin-gle up-front, annual payment (Timing of Cash) making a one-year com-mitment (Length of Commitment), and the deal specifics were mutually aligned around signature during the month (Timing of the Deal).

As Eric continually refreshed his inbox, hoping for a signature notifi-cation from his sponsor, Sharon, an email from her did arrive. However, it wasn't the notification he had hoped for. Instead, Sharon indicated to Eric, "It's down to the final signature, our CFO. He's reviewed every-thing but wants to have a discussion with you before he signs."

So Eric immediately called me, asking if I could participate. "Of course," I responded.

The three of us quickly arranged a conference call (before Zoom's pervasiveness). I was in Chicago, Eric was at his home, and we were planning to do some in-call strategy via direct message during the call. Ben, the client's CFO, was in his office. (I call him Ben here because his phone personality resembled Ben Stein's, the writer and actor known for being very dry and monotone.)

Ben, the CFO, started right in.

"I've reviewed the agreement. It looks good. However, we would like to adjust the agreement to reflect starting with 18,000 consultant licenses instead of 35,000. Can you update the agreement, and I can sign it?"

Out of nowhere, with a tone that felt like you might have to hold a mirror under his nose to see if he was still breathing, an attempt to split Eric's deal in half right at the last minute. Splitting the deal in half would not only have the obvious ramifications of causing forecasts to be missed and compensation to be slashed but would also cost Eric his President's Club attainment—a designation given to the company's top performers, which includes a company-sponsored trip to some exotic location.

I looked down at my direct message app, where Eric was exclaiming the s-word repeatedly: "(Poop! Poop! Poop! Poop!)"

Ben had not been involved in a single discussion to date with us regarding the solution, the pricing, or the contract. He was what I refer to as a helicopter approver, having been hovering around the sales process the entire time, but only dropping in right at the last moment.

Does he care about the "value" of the solution? Of course not.

Does he care about our perspective about why the outcome won't be as great? He would ask his own team for their opinion, not ours.

So, what would you do? In our case, we used the Four Levers.

Step One: Be Human

After listening to his request, I briefly teed up a question: "I understand the ask. Over the past few months, we've been working with the team on the rollout plan, specifically around both the implementation and the education of the 35,000 consultants as reflected. Can you give us some insight into the request to halve that?"

Ben explained in his monotone voice, "Yes, I see the plan. I can see that it will take some time to roll out the solution to the 35,000 consultants, so it makes more sense to start with 18,000, see how it goes, and then add the 17,000 additional consultants later in the year."

Again, Eric DM'd me a series of additional expletives. What would be our comeback?

Now, by being human versus slapping right into an answer, we understood Ben's lens. He, as a CFO, wants to hold on to cash while also reducing business risk. Makes perfect sense.

115

However, simply splitting the transaction in half impacts Ben's overall investment, so it was time to explain it to him.

Step Two: Review All Four Levers

"Okay. Understood. Before we do, our business model and, as such, the price before you is based on four primary levers. Your price is based on Volume, or how many licenses you are committing to. Your price is based on the Timing of Cash, or how fast you are paying for the solution. Your price is based on the Length of Commitment, or how long you are committing to the solution. And your price is based on our mutual alignment of the Timing of the Deal, which we had established with your team. I believe this is similar to the drivers of your organization; you want customers to commit to more Volume, pay faster, commit longer, and help you forecast your business . . ."

I then immediately went into addressing the request. Step Three.

Step Three: Discuss Using All Four Levers

"Regarding these four, your pricing is based on a commitment to 35,000 licenses, paid up front annually NET30, committing to a one-year term, and that mutual alignment around timing is based on a signature tomorrow. We are essentially paying you in the form of a discount in exchange for your mutual assistance in helping us predict the timing. The 35,000-license commitment is important in that your price per license is significantly less than it would be if you were to essentially halve that commitment. Again, we are paying you in the form of favorable per-seat licenses in exchange for that 35,000 commitment. I can have Eric draw up what the price would be if you were to only commit to 18,000 licenses now, then add an additional 17,000 later in the year." I quickly reminded him of the protections in the contract if the solution

116

does not meet expectations via the "Warranty" and "Termination for Cause" provisions.

The phone went silent, and it was hard to tell if Ben was still there or if we had been disconnected.

I immediately direct-messaged Eric: "He needs to be the next one to speak. Put your phone on mute if you have to."

Eric replied via direct message to me: "It already is. Otherwise, he would have heard me moaning."

In what felt like forever, Ben finally responded. "Eric, please send over what the pricing would look like split, versus the up-front commitment."

It has been a few years, but I seem to remember Ben not even saying, "Thank you for the time," or "Goodbye." I think he just hung up!

Eric and I called each other, commiserated, but strategized on providing Ben with the per-license cost at 18,000 seats versus 35,000 seats and how the overall investment would be significantly higher. We sent it over.

Eric didn't sleep well that night. However, the next morning, Ben signed the agreement for the full 35,000 licenses. Later the following month, Eric was onstage at Sales Kickoff and a few weeks later he was basking in the sun at the President's Club trip.

Remember that while your business model is created to reward customers who commit to more, pay faster, commit longer, and help you forecast when people buy things, they typically desire the opposite. Your customers prefer to commit to as little as possible, pay as slowly as possible, not make any commitment at all if they can avoid it, and sign whenever the heck they want. A CFO is this times 10. A CFO desires to minimize commitments and risks while holding cash as long as possible. We have to expect this.

The discussion with Ben was no surprise. However, the Four Levers is a language anyone in an organization can understand. When any of Ben's company's customers desire to halve a Volume commitment, of course, the pricing would have to change. Ben was a professional negotiator, seeking to achieve the goals of his role. The presentation of how the Four Levers were explained, coupled with how the fourth lever specifically, Timing of the Deal, was explained, I believe caused a realization that our pricing was formed on a sound basis, and he didn't have time to mess around. Anytime your customer wants to lower their Volume commitment, return to the levers.

In many cases, the helicopter buyer, who is employed to mess with vendors, is simply seeking to poke the bunny rabbit to see how scared it gets. There are times when individuals who haven't been involved in any of your discussions through the process throw a grenade into a pricing model just to see what happens. And when nothing happens, when the rabbit doesn't flinch, a signature is imminent.

Without a process by which you can stand firmly in your pricing model, any discussion can sound forced, lack confidence, and show the buyer cracks they can attempt to wedge open. There is nothing magical about how I present the Four Levers other than practice. Again, you can do this.

But what if the conversation is not with a CFO but with your program sponsor? This question highlights the importance of Step One: Being Human. It is so important to understand the source of the issue.

In the story above, Ben used a goal-line negotiation tactic. However, if this discussion had taken place with Sharon, not Ben, and two weeks earlier, the issue may have been her confidence in your solution. Asking and understanding the source of the issue is critical, given that if this were simply a *"We're not sure this is going to achieve our desired outcomes,"* you have a sales issue to address, not a negotiation issue.

Volume is the primary driver of your pricing model. Committing to less Volume means paying more for each element within the Volume. Make sure your customers understand the implications of smaller commitments.

"WE NEED TO TRY THIS OUT FOR A LITTLE WHILE, JUST TO SEE HOW IT WORKS IN OUR ENVIRONMENT"

These should be dreaded words in a sales cycle if you sell a solution of any substance.

It often makes sense why a customer might ask to try before they buy. Working this whole thing backward for a moment, I want you to picture the last time you purchased something of substance. Did you make the purchase when (a) you were convinced to buy it; or (b) you made a prediction where the conclusion was, "*Yes, this is the right place to put my time, resources, and dollars versus the other options of where I should put my time, resources, and dollars*"?

Our brains are prediction machines. We don't buy when we're convinced; we buy when we feel we can predict. We buy when that prediction tells us the juice will be worth the squeeze. "*The effort, budget outlay, and opportunity cost are worth the outcome I'm confident I will receive.*"

Okay, now consider this question: When considering buying something of substance, is your prediction ever that "This solution is perfect," "There is nothing that is or could go wrong with this purchase," "There is no trade-off at all . . . this is the mostest perfectest thing on the planet Earth"?

Nope. Never.

We, as human beings, subconsciously know that perfection does not exist. There is always a downside. There is always something being given up. There is always something that isn't perfect.

Okay, let's put our salesperson hat back on.

It is easier than ever for a buyer to predict their experience with your solutions. The proliferation of reviews and feedback on everything is now a fact of life. The ability to connect and network with peers who have potentially experienced your solution is also easier than ever.

If you believe this to be true, our goal should be to get a buyer to an accurate prediction as quickly as possible, right? An accurate prediction that either leads to you or to another solution, right? Win . . . or, if you're going to lose, lose fast.

When a customer asks to do a pilot, it typically means we have missed something along their buying journey. The customer has not reached a confident conclusion in their attempt to *predict* the outcome of using your solution in their environment, and as such, needs to do more research.

Can you blame them?

Our job as sales professionals is to help the buyer predict. The proliferation of reviews and feedback and the ability for your prospects to connect with their peers who have experience addressing similar challenges mean our focus should be on providing the truth. Without truth, without trust, and without delivering confident predictions, the customer is often stuck. What else can they do?

When the customer asks to do a pilot, the three steps for addressing this concession request (because that is what it is) are exactly the same as for other requests.

Step One: Be Human

Ask, "Can you tell me more about why you feel a proof-of-concept/pilot project is your desired path at this point?" Use your own words, but it is important to assess where this request is coming from.

"We need to be sure this will work in our unique environment."

Yes. Yes, they do.

If you are a start-up with a limited number of customers or this customer is in a new category for your business (e.g., a new vertical, geography, market, or revenue tier), you may have to pursue some sort of additional proof.

However, as I work with companies that, in some cases, have thousands of customers, the problem is not their ability to predict. The problem likely lies in our approach to aiding the customer in their prediction.

When discussing this scenario with one of my larger customers, one of the participants said this, which I love: *"As an established organization like we are, there aren't many 'concepts' left to 'prove.'"*

Step Two: Review All Four Levers

Similar to how we handled the Termination for Convenience or out-clause request in an earlier chapter, I do not advise you to tell the customer, *"We don't do pilots."* That may cause a flip in customer trust and trigger an immediate thought of choosing another path. Thinking through empathetic eyes, might this response signal to the customer that you are hiding something? If you are so confident, prove it. Instead, explain it through the lens of the levers.

"I understand. As we have discussed, our business model and your pricing are based on four fundamental levers. And I reviewed them."

Why would we go to the levers here? Because, at its core, a pilot is a short-term Length of Commitment. It should be priced as such.

Step Three: Discuss Using All Four Levers

We should signal to the customer that a pilot or proof-of-concept has a cost associated with it.

Before reviewing all Four Levers, point out to the customer the third lever, Length of Commitment.

"Your pricing is based on an X-year commitment. If you would like to do a short-term pilot, that represents a much shorter commitment, and we will have to look at the pricing and the levers to determine how best to address this."

Now, before they freak out, there are two points worth making:

1. **Other ways to help them reach a strong prediction:** *"At its core, it sounds like we haven't done a great job of helping you predict. Before we go down the path of pricing out and planning for a pilot, where are you stuck?"* Are there other ways you can help them feel comfortable with their decision *for* or even *against* you?

2. **Allocation of resources:** Today, when you engage in a strategic proof-of-concept or pilot project with a customer, what resources are you using to aid the buyer through it? Are they your best resources? Organizations often want to make such a favorable impression to win new revenue that they steer all their best people to the project. Now, ask yourself, *Do we want our best resources to spend their time on our committed customers or our uncommitted ones?* The answer should be simple.

I always wanted my best resources focused on the success of my committed customers. When successful, those committed customers stay, buy more, advocate for our solutions to their peers, and take us with them to their next organizations.

This line has helped many understand the why behind charging for pilots and proofs-of-concept: *"We have to charge for pilot projects because we prefer to allocate our best resources to our committed customers, not our uncommitted ones. Once you are on board, you will get the best we've got. This is why we have had the success we have so far."*

If the customer still wants to do the pilot, the pricing should reflect the Four Levers, just like a larger deal:

- **Volume:** A smaller commitment to your solutions should be priced like any client committing to a smaller amount of Volume.
- **The Timing of Cash** should look exactly like the larger commitment. If it's up front, NET30, the customer should pay up

front, NET30. If they want to change those pricing terms, use the levers as you would in any pricing term discussion.

- **The Length of Commitment** should reflect how long they will need to prove the concept best. If it is a three-month project, pricing should reflect the difference between a customer making a three-month commitment and an annual or multiyear commitment.

- **The Timing of the Deal:** If you are allocating resources to the proof-of-concept, the predictability of when you will need those resources to be available and when they will be ready to roll off the project should be valuable data to your organization. Any concessions for the proof-of-concept or pilot project should keep this in mind.

"WELL, OUR COMPETITORS OFFER PROOFS-OF-CONCEPT"

When we follow our competitors' actions, we are missing opportunities. We are stymying innovation. We have our eye on the wrong ball. Our focus should always be on our customers, not our competitors and what they are doing. If a competitor is offering a proof-of-concept to win a deal, go back to: *"We prefer to allocate our best resources to our committed customers, not our uncommitted ones."*

Then, look back at the agreement. Similar to how we discussed the Termination for Convenience request in chapter 10, your agreement has protections for the customer in terms of:

- **Warranties:** A warranty is a legally binding commitment forming part of the sales contract, which assures the buyer that the product or service is free from defects. A warranty often provides for a specific remedy such as repair or replacement in the event the article or service fails to meet the warranty.[8]

- **Termination for Cause:** A Termination for Cause clause is a contractual provision that allows one or both parties to terminate the agreement due to the occurrence of specific circumstances or events that constitute a material breach or default by the other party.[9]
- **Service-Level Agreements:** A service-level agreement (SLA) defines the level of service expected from a vendor, lays out metrics by which the service is measured, and provides remedies should service levels not be achieved.[10]

In other words, depending on what you sell, if the solution does not perform, you have language in your agreements in at least one of these three areas protecting a customer. The customer can either terminate the agreement or have remedies to resolve the issue. It is okay to remind the customer that these protections exist.

"WE HAVE A FREE PILOT ON OUR WEBSITE ALREADY—IT IS A GREAT SOURCE OF LEADS"

To start, ask yourself two questions:

1) What percentage of prospects who engage in your free pilot on the website convert to a paying customer?

Imagine if you had a store that gave away free samples. One hundred people walked through the doors of your store and tried the samples. Seventy-five of those people left, never buying anything, and never returned. The problem is that we often view the 25 people who did buy as a win. However, 75 people tried it, did not like it, and you never heard from them again. Three-fourths of those experiencing your product invested their attention, interest, and time and were not impressed enough to pay for it.

Do you know why? Do you care? You should.

Even if the spread is 40% buy, 60% don't, there is a significant opportunity being missed. More importantly, 60% of people trying your product in your store are now telling their friends, *"Meh, I wouldn't go there. I tried it. It wasn't great."* The 60% is multiplying without you even knowing it.

Remember, every single lead has a cost. That cost could be in the form of your and your team's time attending to it, chasing it, and attempting to convert it into a paying customer.

2) What percentage of those who convert to paying customers stay?

Do you know how many of your customers who tried your solution liked it enough to buy it and stayed beyond their initial commitment term? In other words, does the pilot experience create an accurate lens to a prediction for the customer? Does the pilot experience create accurate expectations?

When customers try, buy, and then leave, two primary issues are happening:

- First, those customers often are the ones who are hogging your resources. With many experiencing problems in their environment, which result in ultimately going in another direction when their term expires, it means something is not clicking. The customer is calling support, likely upset. Your costs to serve the customer have gone up because reality did not meet the expectation set during the free trial period. In other words, unless your solution converts a very high percentage of free trials into paying customers who stay, it may be worth assessing the cost of serving those customers.

- Second, the most significant development in the world of information availability to your buyers is the proliferation of reviews and feedback on everything we do, buy, and experience. Before Amazon started collecting and displaying reviews right under their own products on their own websites in the mid-1990s,[11] the path for a customer to share their dissatisfaction was limited. Today, regardless of the product you are selling, the accessibility of information on customers' experiences can be of massive value or a considerable detriment to future sales.

Consider the experience you are creating for those who walk in your doors. Optimize the experience, and treat pilots or proofs-of-concept as you would a short-term commitment.

CHAPTER 14

Trou-Dropping Competitors and Ridiculous Discounts

The old adage "You can sell anything if you make the price low enough" can be reversed and applied with equal force, "You can secure any price if you make the article good enough." The salesman who believes in his article should feel confident whether the price is a high one or not.
—M. S. Burton, Salesmanship Magazine, 1906

When a salesman writes an order at a cut price concession, he's putting himself in the buyer's power in all future dealings.
—Henderson Foulke, The Cord Age, 1927

THE TROU-DROPPING COMPETITOR

"We have a competitor that always drops trou right at the goal line against us, willing to buy the business to win deals away from us."

"Drop trou" is the technical term for drastically dropping price in order to either buy business away from a competitor or force the competitor's price down to damage their profit margin.

In preparation for any negotiation program I am delivering for a client, we have a preparatory call to understand their pricing model, the language around the levers, and the challenges they continually face when negotiating with their clients. At the end of the call, I conduct what I refer to as a "lightning round," during which I predict the top eight items clients ask for (or demand) during a negotiation. I'm typically correct around 95% of the time. In almost all of the cases, the client has a low-cost competitor or one who seemingly doesn't care about margins and is willing to do anything to win.

"It drives us crazy. They do it every time!"

Some companies seemingly believe that when all else fails, they should lower the price so much that the decision for the buyer is easy. They believe any revenue is good revenue; having clients at all is better than having none. These low-cost competitors believe that they are winning when, in fact, they are losing.

There is a quote often attributed to English polymath John Ruskin in the 1800s that I believe most of us would agree with:

It is unwise to pay too much, but it is worse to pay too little. When you pay too much, you lose a little money—that's all. When you pay too little, you sometimes lose everything, because the thing you bought was incapable of doing the thing it was bought to do. The common law of business balance prohibits paying a little and getting a lot—it can't be done. If you deal with the lowest bidder, it is well to add something for the risk you run, and if you do that you will have enough to pay for something better.

We, as selling professionals, give so much power to the price-cutting competitor, when, in fact, the price-cutting competitor cuts their own power. Your buyer does not want a price that's lower than everyone else's price. Your buyer wants an equitable price that matches the value they are receiving in return, in line with what other companies who are making a purchase from you are receiving. You can accelerate the decline of your competitor's power by setting expectations up front.

Isn't it amazing when you talk to someone who can consistently predict the future? They earn instant credibility. As a baseball fan, there is an analyst who did television broadcasts for the Chicago Cubs for many years and is now the analyst on television for the Chicago White Sox. Steve Stone is a former major-league pitcher, and what is incredible is how he can predict the next pitch the pitcher will throw: "In this situation, after throwing a curveball low and outside, he will now throw a fastball to the inside portion of the plate, which will either cause the batter to watch strike three without swinging or, if he can make contact, it will be weak contact on the barrel of the bat." Suddenly, the pitcher throws the inside fastball; the batter just stares at it and the umpire says, "Strike three!" The batter is out. You think, *This person really knows their stuff!*

Similar to an expert on TV, you can build that same credibility by predicting what your competitor will do. When expectations are set correctly and your competitors "drop trou" during the process, your prospective customer is ready for it. They are considerably less likely to come to you later in the process asking for a ridiculous discount due to a competitor attempting to buy the business. They already know the price, have been preparing for it, and know exactly how it is determined.

During the "positioning your pricing" conversation we discussed in chapter 6, set the competitive trou-dropping expectation, but not in a "rip the competitor" type of way. Instead, say something like this: *"Based on our understanding of your environment and needs, your price will likely be between $X and $Y. As we continue to get to know each other, we'll hone this, and you'll understand why our customers pay this amount.*

"There are other, less expensive options. In some cases, competitors are willing to take business at a loss. If that sounds attractive, and price will be the primary driver, can we discuss that now versus later?"

I have heard a few of my clients actually joke with their prospects: *"If price is going to be everything here, we can give you a quote you can run over to them right now. We don't mind."*

In other words:

1. Would you rather lose to an aggressive competitor during the first call or the twentieth? Lose fast. Unless you are an early-stage company with no customers, there is a reason why your customers pay what they do. By setting that expectation early, you are maximizing your most valuable asset—your time.

   > The successful salesman hoards minutes and hours as a miser hoards gold. The spendthrift of time is a sure candidate for failure.
   > —Worthington C. Holman, *Ginger Talks*, 1908

2. Disarm the competitive move: To the point above regarding the baseball analyst, when the competitor does drop their price aggressively, the thought is not, *Oooh, I can use this to pound (you) into price submission.* Instead, it's, *Oh, jeez. Yep. Sure enough, my salesperson was right.* How can that customer possibly come to you with the competitor's aggressive price if the issue was discussed at the beginning of the sales process?

   And if the customer were to say, *"Yes, as you perfectly predicted, your competitor has come in 50% lower than you. Can you do anything?"* your answer can and should be the Four Levers. You can treat it like a discount request.

> Everything else being equal, a customer buys where he
> can buy cheapest. . . . Everything is not equal.
> —James Samuel Knox, *Salesmanship*
> *and Business Efficiency,* 1915

Establish the expectation up front. Your value will shine. And you'll disarm your competitor before they can "drop trou."

THE MASSIVE DISCOUNT ASK

"In doing our homework, we have found an alternative solution that is dramatically less expensive than yours. I cannot possibly justify paying your price when this is the case. We like you and your solution, but the price will need to come down 50% for us to move forward."

What do you do?

First, as discussed previously, setting the expectation up front that your product is not the least expensive option on the market is the quickest way to disarm this conversation before it happens. For one of my larger clients, their solution is at the top of the market in terms of price and capabilities. They have a number of smaller competitors who are trying to get their foot in the door and, as a result, are certainly going to be lower priced. This client mentions this fact during the first conversation with the client. As a result, what I refer to as the "ridiculous discount ask" rarely comes up.

However, if

a. we have not set that expectation early,

b. we are working with a buying team where others on the team have found this alternative, not being privy to that earlier conversation,

c. the client has genuinely found an alternative that they believe can address the issue, or

d. we have a customer who wants to "see what they can get" by throwing a negotiation grenade into the mix late . . .

. . . we must be prepared for the conversation.

For the most part, this quote from an interview with a procurement manager in a 1931 edition of *Sales Management* magazine captures typical buyer behavior well, especially where you have built any trusting relationship:

> Our success depends on our ability to get the lowest price quoted on the goods we handle. We do not want a better price. We have never asked any manufacturer to give us a better price than he gives to other carload buyers. On an equal price basis, how to get an equitable price is the most serious problem which faces our business.[12]
>
> —*Sales Management* magazine, 1931

Step One: Be Human

Just like any of the other concession requests, this response should be handled in a similar fashion: Understand the source of the request. "*Oh, wow. Congratulations!*" might sound like a snarky response. Still, when a customer believes they can achieve their desired outcome at a fraction of the cost, if your perspective on being a sales professional is being a true partner (guiding the customer to achieve their goals with or without you), you should be excited for them. "*Tell me more. Is there an alternative that will get you to your outcome effectively that's considerably less expensive?*" Then listen.

If you had set the expectation for the customer earlier in the process, you could certainly start the conversation with, "*As we discussed, there are alternatives that are less expensive than us, but that much?*"

Step Two: Review All Four Levers

It is okay to walk away. And your confidence in the delivery of that message is important.

"As you recall, our pricing model is based on how much you buy [Volume], how fast you pay [Timing of Cash], how long you commit [Length of Commitment], and when you sign [Timing of the Deal]."

Then, roll immediately into the conversation around the concession request.

Step Three: Discuss Using All Four Levers

"We can walk through the levers again to see how close we can get. Unfortunately, we can't get anywhere close to their pricing. If that price is where you need to get to, we wish you the best of luck. It's been a pleasure working with you."

Your confidence and willingness to walk away are often the greatest customer magnet.

> Mr. Customer thinks you lack the sand to stick to your proper
> price. Don't give in. Don't lose your nerve. Hang on—stick
> tight—hold fast to the legitimate selling price. Don't come out
> at the little end of the horn.
>
> —*Salesmanship Magazine*, 1906[13]
> (quote and image on next page)

Not all revenue is good revenue. In a business-to-business environment, where your goal is often to not only close the transaction but also get the customer to stay, buy more, and become an advocate for you, profit erodes the minute you give in even a little. More importantly, it is also the minute their confidence and trust in your pricing model erodes with it.

THE SMALL END OF THE HORN

Your role is to aid the buyer. If they have truly found a solution that addresses their desired outcomes for a significantly lower investment than your solution provides, learn from it and feel good for the customer. *"Our solution is way too much for them—in terms of functionality and in terms of price."* In the words of the greatest sales philosopher of all time, in my opinion, Arthur Sheldon:

True salesmanship is the science of service. Grasp that thought firmly and never let go.

—Arthur Sheldon, *The Art of Selling*, 1911

CHAPTER 15

The Legal Stuff

Simplify the contract. . . . It should usually be simple
and short. The buyer has no time to puzzle out a
complicated legal document and search for the
"joker" which he suspects is concealed therein.
—*Frederic Arthur Russell*, Textbook
of Salesmanship, *1924*

Until this point in the book, we have been almost solely focused on the commercial or deal terms of an agreement. Our aim has been to help you build trust, discount less, improve your forecasting accuracy, and do all of this in a simple, confident way. But what happens after the customer says yes?

In most cases, we load up a contract, master services agreement, licensing agreement, or similar, launch it over, and the customer replies, *"We have submitted this to our procurement/legal team."*

Then we wait. And wait. And wait some more.

Finally, there is a response. *"Our legal team has some redlines for you to review."* Then, the back-and-forth begins.

We have lost control of the process. The momentum the buyer feels for achieving their desired outcomes has slowed, and in many cases, the contract process itself erodes mutual trust.

LAWYERS ARE PEOPLE TOO

There. I said it. Lawyers are human beings. Hearts that beat. Lungs that breathe. And brains that are designed precisely the same as yours.

Your end-of-quarter or end-of-month is stressful. You are trying to close all of the transactions you are working on. The deals all seem to slide to the end of the month or quarter, don't they? How about your customer's lawyers? Theoretically, wouldn't this mean legal teams are piled higher with agreements to review at the end of the month and quarter too?

Your manager asks you, the salesperson, for status updates on your deals more frequently at the end of the fiscal period. You then ask your customer sponsor for an update. Your sponsor then pings the legal team. Multiply that by however many contracts a customer's legal team is being asked to review and "approve by the end of the month for signature."

Let's imagine the pile of contracts sitting on the lawyer's desk. They grab one and immediately see it is filled with words like *heretofore*, *whereas*, and *notwithstanding*. Their brains cry a little on the inside. The goal for the lawyer? Find the gotchas—the things the vendor hopes you don't notice—and the items intentionally placed in the agreement to serve as chips during the give-and-take discussions.

The bumpier the road, the slower the drive. Yet, the traditional approach to the legal formality stage of the sales process is designed to add bumps to the road. We have created a process to put the customer's legal team on the defensive while also writing contracts in a way no human being would want to read if it were not their job to do so.

> We are not thinking machines that feel, we are feeling machines that think.
>
> —António R. Damásio

When moving up into a C-level role, this thought hit me. Having been on the sales end of the table for my entire career, the contracts and legal stage was just something that needed to happen. However, moving to the other side of the table, where I had to understand agreements while running my own business, I am like the paralegal having to review any contract before signing. My perspective shifted.

There's an opportunity. How can we create contracts lawyers want to read? How do we build trust with lawyers versus eroding it? How do we pave the road, thereby speeding the review and accompanying legalese negotiation?

1) Be Human

Can we challenge the notion that our legal contracts need to be written in a way no human being would ever speak?

My speaking/training agreement has jokes in it. Well, not really jokes, but promises like my lack of need for any crazy green room requests—no special ferns, sticks of butter (I've seen this before), certain colored M&M's, or aromatherapy candles. The first two words of my agreements are "Thank you": "*Thank you for considering me to be a resource for you and your team.*"

My agreements speed through legal and rarely get marked up. I've got to believe this is partially due to the fact that I've tried to make it the easy stop . . . not the hard one. It speeds to the top of the pile.

"We are feeling machines that think." When we meet someone with a smile, it makes us smile. We are not immediately on the defensive. Smiles build trust. Make your agreements smile.

2) Smooth the Road

Are there terms that get redlined every single time you send them to a customer? One-way, selfish terms that only benefit you, the selling organization? The second a lawyer sees one of these terms, the second a lawyer must cross out and comment on an unacceptable clause in an agreement, is the moment their brain's alert system is activated. A lawyer immediately knows they have to read every single word carefully. *What other gotchas have they hidden in here?* is the immediate thought.

Terms like "automatic price increases," "automatic renewals," "commitments to do marketing and/or a case study" are terms you know will give the customer heartburn. Either remove them, adjust the wording and intent to be mutually valuable, or see the third idea below.

3) The Legal Cover Sheet

Don't want to add personality to your contracts? I understand. However, you can guide the lawyer in the agreements you send. Try attaching a simple, easy-to-read, bulleted cover letter to the agreement. Add your personality in an unofficial cover letter.

Start with a thank-you: *"Thank you for taking the time to review our agreement."*

"While we are probably biased in our view, we have put together this agreement to be the simplest one you review this week."

Then, point out the areas where lawyers get stuck or where context can help shape the lens by which they view the terms.

For example, in my own agreements, I call out a few areas that, without context, can slow things down:

1. **The Four Levers:** In my agreements, I have four bullets under "Payment" that explain the levers succinctly. Why are these in the contract? Because the lawyers or procurement representatives may not have been involved in the discussions to date and may challenge the price, the term length, or, most often, the payment terms.

2. **The Timing of Cash:** I explain in the agreement note that my business is based on aligning payments with the outlay of my time. The programs I deliver require my time in real time with the client. This heads off their *"Our standard payment terms are NET60"* before they ask.

3. **Cancellation:** I explain in the note why my termination provision is written as it is. Given that I exchange my time for dollars, in a case where a client desires to cancel before the program is delivered, there's an associated payment that will still be due. This is based on my ability to reassign my time for dollars. Without that context, the lawyers may seek to change the cancellation clause.

4. **Anything Nonstandard for the Industry:** Are there any elements of your agreement that are different from those of your competitors, or in the case of replacing an incumbent, which are different from theirs? For example, in one of my previous organizations, the incumbents' Timing of Cash was typically billed monthly. Ours was annual. When we set that expectation up front, objections were dissolved before the agreement was ever sent. If not addressed beforehand, make sure it's called out clearly on the cover.

In my own business today, there are two things I do that most other practitioners do not.

1. I encourage you to record the training workshops I teach (for internal use) for no extra charge. I want it to become an internal training asset—part of your culture. It is in the contract, and I call it out on the cover.
2. If you record the program, I'd like a copy, but I understand if you don't want to share it.

Imagine reading an engaging cover sheet with a few short, bulleted items that provide context and personality before digging into the legal mumbo jumbo of an agreement. Wouldn't it make it easier to read? Wouldn't it make you want to prioritize the agreement with the cover sheet ahead of the others? Wouldn't it save a great deal of time? Lawyers get endorphins from checking items off their to-do lists or completing tasks just like other human beings.

In my experience, whether with my own company or previous organizations, adding personality to the agreement or via a cover note resulted in the legal negotiation stage being shortened, redlines being reduced, trust growing, and customers achieving their desired outcomes faster.

SALES ROLE IN LEGAL LANGUAGE

How often have you clicked "accept" when asked to accept the terms of some product you are about to use without reading the language you are accepting? The operating system on your computer probably asked you to click through an end-user license agreement (EULA), and your video game system, like PlayStation or Xbox, likely did the same. Have a gym membership? Guessing you signed an agreement before your first workout. Your credit card applications have them, and even those renting an e-scooter accepted an agreement before scooting around town.

Did you actually read the terms? I'm guessing one or two of you said yes. But the rest? Probably not.

But why didn't you?

Is it learned helplessness—meaning, if you find a term you disagree with, you are helpless to do anything about it?

Is it blind trust—meaning, if many people use a product, they all likely had to agree to these terms so that social proof tells us it must be okay?

Is it the length of the agreements? Nobody has time to read all that, right? The complex legalese?

Is it the take-it-or-leave-it dilemma? If you don't accept, you can't use whatever it is you want to use.

In 2015, as my family readied for a trip to the Happiest Place on Earth, Disneyland in California, we boarded our two dogs at a local dog hotel. As we were walking into the park for the first time, the phone rang. The dog hotel lost one of our dogs. (The story gets much more intense, which I describe in my first book, *The Transparency Sale*, in the afterword.) We eventually filed suit against the boarding facility for the costs associated with the search. However, the boarding facility had a "Limitation of Liability" clause in the agreement, which I signed before the first time we used the facility. I don't remember signing it, but I clearly did. It capped their liability for those costs at $500.

Given that the boarding facility acted in bad faith throughout the search, we settled at a higher amount, but now, many years later, I read through every agreement with every meaningful product. While we could have never imagined this scenario with our beloved Digger happening, this is exactly why lawyers read your agreements on high alert. Lawyers have to imagine every scenario, every worst case, and picture the company they represent in those scenarios.

Lawyers protect the business. They ensure compliance. They seek fairness. They reduce risk. They solve disputes. They shield your business's intellectual property. In many cases, the lawyer's job is made more difficult because organizations who sell to them have taught them to find the gotchas in their agreements.

With this in mind, the salesperson has a role in making your legal team's life easier.

Your pricing model is based on how much Volume a customer commits to, the Timing of Cash, the Length of Commitment your customer makes, and predictability through the Timing of the Deal. However, your business and pricing model is also run under the assumption of a *reasonable amount of risk*.

While you have likely settled on the agreement's terms, what happens when your customer's legal team asks for special language concessions?

First, engage your own counsel in any discussions with opposing counsel. Do not try to handle legalese concession discussions and language edits yourself.

Second, you can include the Four Levers in setting up a discussion to set expectations for your customer contact.

When selling to highly regulated companies, where you know legal will be a challenge, adding a comment to the end of your pricing positioning is a good place to start.

"Our pricing is based on Four Levers." Go on to share the four: (1) How much you buy (Volume). (2) How fast you pay (Timing of Cash). (3) How long you commit (Length of Commitment). (4) When you sign (Timing of the Deal).

Add the sentence, *"The pricing is also based on accepting a reasonable level of risk . . ."*

As the negotiation of legal language is taking place, unless you have a law degree and license, let your lawyer be the one speaking to their lawyer. However, when the client asks for unreasonable levels of indemnification exposure, liability limits, nonstandard service level commitments, massive amounts of insurance, or a number of other requests, reminding the client of the sentence can be helpful.

"As we work through this language, remember that our pricing is based on the Four Levers, assuming an acceptable level of risk commensurate with our other clients." In other words, it may turn out that these concessions are items you, the customer, must pay us to accept.

COMMON LEGALESE TERMS EXPLAINED

It took me years to understand what the word *indemnification* actually means. What are Warranties, liabilities in a business sense, and service-level agreements? Here's a quick summary.

In most agreements, there is certain legal language that exists to guide in circumstances where things go wrong. What happens if the product you sell doesn't do what the customer is signing up for? What happens if the product you are selling damages property, people, and reputations? What happens if proprietary information gets into the hands of competitors, or secrets are leaked that create problems for those who have been exposed? What are the remedies? How much time do you have to provide the remedy? If you have to go to court, how will that occur, and where?

For simplicity's sake, let's talk through some of the terms you may hear.

Indemnification

Let's say you borrow your neighbor's lawn mower. You probably don't have a written agreement covering damages to the lawn mower itself or because of the lawn mower, but you are essentially indemnifying the owner. If you break the neighbor's lawn mower while using it, you agree to pay for the repairs. If, while using the lawn mower, you run over a branch that flies through another person's window, you are agreeing to pay for the damages. Indemnification is a fancy term for the promise to pay for anything that goes wrong.

Limitation of Liability

This clause limits how much you, the solution provider, will pay if something goes wrong. For example, if you sold someone a bicycle, limitation of liability language might say, "If a part breaks, we aren't paying for the award you missed out on because you lost the bike race." Or to take that further, you aren't going to be paying for hospital bills if the individual happens to fall off the bike.

What's the difference? Imagine you have rented a car:

- Indemnification says that if you crash into someone or something, you pay the damages you have caused, not the rental car company.
- The limitation of liability states that if the car breaks down while you are using it, the company will pay the rental car costs but won't pay for the flight you missed because the car stalled.

In one case, while running the revenue organization for a ratings and reviews provider, we sold to one of the largest mobile wireless providers in the United States. The wireless company would use our technology to collect and display ratings and reviews on their website alongside each product they sold. After agreeing to commercial terms, the agreement went to legal, eventually stalling. This organization demanded in the agreement that if a product or service customer review showed up on their website, collected via an unverified source, was deemed untrue, and damaged their reputation, we would be responsible for an uncapped amount of lost revenue. In other words, a multibillion-dollar organization demanded that our organization, doing less than US$30M in revenue at the time, would pay unlimited damages to their reputation caused by a single false review.

This client and deal would have been a huge opportunity for our organization, and specifically for our salesperson working it.

We explained to the organization that while the scenario was incredibly unlikely to ever happen, our pricing and entire business model couldn't survive such an instance. Also, the amount of insurance we would need to procure to cover such a scenario would render the agreement unprofitable and not worth pursuing. Again, our pricing model is based on the Four Levers, assuming an acceptable level of risk commensurate with our other clients. In this case, the level of risk was not acceptable and nowhere near commensurate with our other clients.

Unfortunately, we could not come to an agreement and had to walk away from this opportunity.

Handling Legal Language Concession Requests

Even in simple, small business-to-business transactions, your clients may ask for nonstandard protections. In my own business, I have had clients ask me for what I would call ridiculous levels of insurance protection. I would be coming on-site to do a half-day workshop, followed by some virtual reinforcement activities. Yet, in this example, the client asked me to have $10M worth of insurance protection spread across three policies.

When I follow the three steps for handling legal language concession requests, more often than not, the request disappears.

Step One: Be Human

"In reviewing the agreement and your requests regarding the requirement for me to possess (X, Y & Z) insurance policies, can you tell me a little more about why that's important given our engagement?"

This question alone has caused companies to simply remove them.

"Oh, Todd, sorry. This is standard language we add for all third-party service agreements. This doesn't apply. Can you just send us confirmation of the policies you do have?"

The request is gone.

However, if the request persists beyond your asking for clarification, move on to Step Two.

Step Two: Review All Four Levers

"As we have discussed, our business model, specifically the pricing, is based on Four Levers . . ." (Then, explain the levers briefly as we have done in previous chapters.)

Add, *"The pricing also assumes terms that are commensurate with what our customer base typically requires."*

Step Three: Discuss Using All Four Levers

"As a small business, my pricing is based on having insurance policies, which I do have, commensurate with the reasonable level of risk associated with this program. If you require me to procure this level of insurance, this would require a significant additional investment, which would likely only apply in this engagement with you. As a result, the pricing would have to change to reflect that additional investment."

Then, be quiet and let them respond. Listen.

When delivering programs, more than once, leaders among the participants replied, *"We should just say no."* Be careful. The goal is to learn, collaborate, and build on the trust foundation you have already established. Following this process, I learned from my clients, especially as I began to work with much larger clients and as additional regulations were added that I may not have been paying attention to. Certain requests came up more often and became the standard for those types of engagements.

Begin with a human conversation, where you listen to the reason behind the ask. Explain the "why" behind your pushback using the levers, and you will have much more fruitful, collaborative, and trust-building conversations.

"WE WANT TO USE OUR CONTRACT"

You are selling a product or service to a customer. You send over your agreement, likely explicitly written for the type of product or services you will be delivering. A few days pass, and suddenly, you receive an email from the client that reads, *"We require all of our vendors to use our standard agreement."*

The larger the transaction and the larger the company you are selling to, the more often this concession request is made. You may be reading this and assume you know why the customer requests the use of their agreement versus yours. Are you sure? Follow the three steps for handling concession requests to listen, confirm, and continue to build trust.

Step One: Be Human

"What is the driver behind why your organization requires using your agreement versus ours?" Again, use your own words here, but be a human. Seek to understand what is driving their desire to throw your agreement in the recycle bin and use theirs instead.

It could be any number of reasons, including but not limited to:

- **Negotiation Position:** Some organizations believe forcing you to negotiate based on their language puts themselves in a stronger position than having to negotiate using your language.

147

- **Familiarity:** The lawyers know their own standards. They often believe that using their own agreement saves them time and minimizes risk compared to reviewing an agreement from scratch.
- **Managing Risk:** Larger organizations used to traditional conflict-heavy negotiations desire terms that favor their own business.
- **Compliance:** In heavily regulated industries, there are often standard legal or compliance language requirements that must exist in every agreement.
- **Because They Can:** "We're big. You're small. If you want to do business with us, follow our rules."

Based on their answer, you may, in fact, be stuck having to use their agreement. However, following the discussion around their drivers, explain the why behind *your* drivers.

Step Two: Review All Four Levers

You are probably sick of hearing this response repeatedly, but it's important to remind your customers. In this case, there's an approach to driving the conversation toward a mutual outcome, and it involves your business model. So, just as we have reviewed, *"As we have discussed, our business model, specifically the pricing, is based on Four Levers . . ."* Similar to the previous section discussing the conversation to be had when a client asks you to assume extraordinary levels of risk or added cost, the same can be said here: *"While our pricing is based on those levers, it also assumes a standard legal process."*

Step Three: Discuss Using All Four Levers

There is a cost to you and your business to start from scratch using their agreement. Lawyers aren't cheap. If you have built a good amount of trust through the selling cycle, and specifically in conversations around your commercial and legal terms, explain the "why" in terms of cost. *"Our pricing model is based on those four elements. For us to engage with your agreement, there are added costs we will have to incur. We can do so, but we must adjust something in the commercial terms accordingly."*

Would your organization be willing to use the customer's agreement as a starting point in exchange for a larger investment? More Volume? Faster Timing of Cash? A longer Length of Commitment? Forecast alignment through the Timing of the Deal?

In my business, a couple of my larger clients have requested the use of their agreement. What I have described above is exactly the approach I have taken, explaining, *"I do not have a lawyer on staff. Given the size of this engagement and the associated pricing, if I have to retain legal counsel to review an agreement, the value of this engagement goes out of balance."* While I may be biased in my perspective, based on the trust built up through the process with my clients, one of two things happens:

1. The sponsor pushes back on their own legal department, and my agreement ends up being the one we use. I have written my agreement in conjunction with legal counsel to be engaging, simple, and focused entirely on what I am delivering.
2. The sponsor pushes back on their legal, who, in the instances of compliance requirements, insists on having some standard language added to my agreement.

None of these approaches is foolproof. However, the goal is to understand the why, communicate the why from your organization's perspective, and have trust-building conversations versus animosity-building ones. In many cases, the customer will either concede, offer their own assistance, or, in some cases, pay for it in dollars or in the form of one of the Four Levers.

CHAPTER 16

Quick Hits

*Simple genuineness, transparency of character,
will win the confidence of a customer whether
he is prejudiced or not, and the confidence
of the purchaser is half the sale.*
—*Orison Swett Marden, Selling Things, 1916*

Having talked about, taught, implemented, and used the Four Levers for well over a decade, there are a few things that seem to come up often. Things you may be thinking about in order to adjust the Four Levers for your environment. This chapter, affectionately called "Quick Hits," is dedicated to those ideas in order to help you optimize their use.

IDEA #1: ELIMINATING LEVERS

Having read to this point, you likely have some thoughts swimming around in your head regarding the Four Levers, and how applying them might pertain to your environment. As I've taught Four Levers workshops, I hear things like:

- "Only three of these levers matter to us, because . . ."
- "We don't get paid for a client paying us faster so that lever does not apply."
- "If a client wants to pay NET60 instead of NET30, we can normally get that approved, so we tend to let them."
- "Our solution is very sticky, so shorter commitments are fine."
- "Our solution lends itself to 'land-and-expand,' so a small commitment will grow into something larger anyway."

Let's say you are working on a transaction where the proposal states the client will be paying $20,000 for a specified number of locations, and the solution requires a commitment of at least one year. You get paid based on the dollar amount of the transaction, and while the minimum commitment length is one year, you are bonused for a longer-term commitment. In other words, your compensation is aligned to the Volume and Length of Commitment levers, but does not reward or penalize you for the Timing of Cash lever.

The client, during the negotiation, states, "We require NET60 payment terms in all of our vendor contracts." Your proposal stated payment terms of NET30. You think, *Well, I don't really care about that.* You tell the client, *"Okay. As long as our CFO approves it, we are fine."* No harm to your compensation, right?

Given that you get paid for the dollar amount of the transaction and the commitment length, you have just missed an opportunity to get paid more based on the Timing of Cash.

As discussed in chapter 3, if you have laid the foundation for all Four Levers early, you could trade those payment terms for something you get paid for: *"As you may recall, your pricing is based on how much you buy, how fast you pay, how long you commit, and alignment around the timing of when you will sign. The Timing of Cash is annual up-front payments with NET30 pricing terms. If you'd like to extend the payment terms to NET60, you can, but something else in the agreement must be adjusted to make up for that."*

This does not mean the client should be paying additional cash for the slower payment terms, but might they be willing to commit to an additional year in exchange for NET60 terms? Might they be willing to commit to a few more locations now in exchange for NET60 payment terms?

In my business, my larger clients seemingly always ask for extended payment terms. Most of the time, they do so right before signature. After repeating the levers to my clients, I often add, *"My business is structured in a way where payment needs to be aligned to program delivery. My pricing is configured with that in mind. If you want NET60 payment terms, we can work through that. However, it would require either paying a larger percentage of the program up front, adding additional programs, or committing to a longer engagement."*

The funny thing is, the overwhelming majority of the time I respond in that manner, the client abandons their requirement for NET60 payment terms. In one instance, Bryan, the sales enablement leader for one of my clients, immediately responded, "NET30 is fine." And the request went away as easily as that. However, if slower payment terms were a significant requirement for the client, and if the client was considering additional programs or a longer commitment, I would have missed an opportunity to exchange slower payment terms for something I do get paid for.

All Four Levers are applicable in any business-to-business selling environment. If you do not set all four, you miss an opportunity to trade their ask for something truly meaningful to your business and your compensation.

The same thinking should be considered for your "sticky" solution or your "land-and-expand" business model, where the Length of Commitment lever may feel less important. Can you trade their ask for a shorter commitment, which may feel insignificant to your organization or your personal measures, for something you get paid for? In most instances, using the Four Levers coupled with a sound business explanation, the answer is yes.

What about onetime purchases, where that "Length of Commitment" lever does not seemingly exist? For example, selling real estate. If you are selling real estate, how would the Four Levers apply?

- **Volume:** Certainly the size of the property, the proximity to distribution channels, and the proximity to customers, supplies, or a workforce impact the price. The larger and better, the higher the price. If you can't spend that much, maybe you have to temper your expectations of what you can truly afford regarding the "Volume" of stuff.

- **Timing of Cash:** The dollar amount you end up paying for a home is commensurate with how long you plan to pay for it. A 30-year mortgage will certainly cost you more over that period than a 15-year. Pay cash up front, and you'll pay less.

- **Length of Commitment:** This one may be tricky. It may not apply to a onetime real estate transaction, unless you're selling a lease for the property. I have also seen organizations where the strategic importance of the property to nearby properties impacts a requirement to commit to its use for a period of time.

- **Timing of the Deal:** In a real estate transaction, speed certainly is valued. But, more importantly for the selling party, the ability to predict when "closing" will happen is highly valuable because it allows the seller to plan. Contingencies in purchases should have a price associated with them, whether in dollars or some other element.

Don't overlook a lever because you feel you don't get paid for it anyway or your company doesn't care. When you set all Four Levers, they become the means to not only protect against buyers who are always asking for more but also to allow you to trade for the things you do care about and get paid for.

IDEA #2: ADDING A LEVER: TESTIMONIAL CASE STUDIES

You may be thinking, *We should add a fifth lever. We will tell the customer we'll give them a discount in exchange for committing to publish a testimonial case study with them.* A testimonial case study is a short story from a theoretically happy customer that shows how your product or service helped solve a problem—used to show proof that it works for others like the prospect.

There are three reasons why I strongly disagree with this idea:

1. Paying for case studies erodes trust.
2. Case studies aren't worth the investment.
3. Case study language in an agreement has no teeth.

Paying for Case Studies Erodes Trust

You are renovating your kitchen. It's a considerable investment. These individuals will be traipsing through your home for weeks. You're not just selecting the most skilled contractor or the least expensive contractor; you're also trying to find a dependable, trustworthy human being. So, you have sought out multiple quotations from contractors and narrowed down your choice to a select few.

You do your homework, find reviews to read, and ask the contractors to provide a couple of past clients as references.

One of the contractors has glowing case studies on their website, and the customers they connected you to spoke glowingly of the entire experience. You've made your decision.

However, just as you are about to sign on the dotted line with your selected contractor, you find out that all of the customer testimonials on their website and all of the references you spoke to were paid to provide their 5-star-esque feedback.

How would that make you feel about your selection? Not very good, right?

Imagine being that prospective client, negotiating the final pricing and terms of a deal with you. Depending on the complexity of your deals, they have likely been provided with references. They have likely been provided with testimonial case studies from you too. Aren't you telling the client, "Hey, you know those case studies you read and references you spoke to? The ones that helped you choose us? Yep—we paid those clients for their willingness to provide those, just like we're offering to do with you."

Don't leave your customers questioning the tools they leveraged in order to get to the negotiation stage of the buying process with you.

Case Studies Aren't Worth the Investment

When you are buying something online of substance—meaning, not groceries or daily consumer goods, but something requiring consideration that you have never bought before—do you read the reviews first? At last count, 99% of us do.[14]

However, when buying a mattress, for example, and you see thousands of reviews, and they are all perfect 5-star scored, does your brain think, *Wow. The perfect mattress. Nobody who has ever bought one of these has had anything but a perfect experience, and thus, I will have a perfect experience too?* Or does your brain think, *Something stinks. This company is obviously hiding something, suppressing the negative reviews, and it is possible that all of these reviews are made up?*

Up to 99% of us read reviews before making a purchase, but more importantly, 82% of us read the negative reviews first—the 4-, 3-, 2-, and 1-star ones. A product with an average review score between 4.2 and 4.5 sells better[15] than a product with nothing but perfect 5-star reviews. Negative reviews next to a product on a website help those products sell—because they aid in the buying brain's need for an accurate prediction of what their experience is going to be with those products.

The same is true in human-to-human or business-to-business selling. We know subconsciously that perfection does not exist. Our brains do not buy a product when we are convinced. Or, if we are convinced, we will likely be upset about our purchase soon after. We buy when we can predict. We are prediction machines. We need the negative aspects of a purchase, and trust is built when those negative aspects are presented first. The risks. The pricing range. What a competitor potentially does better than you. Where things have gone wrong in the past.

This is not to say that you should always present your solutions by beginning with the phrase, *"Hey, Mrs. Customer, this is why we suck."* No, the 4.2–4.5-star range is important. Positioning your solutions as not all things to all people builds trust, speeds decision-making, leads to better qualification in and out, and helps you differentiate in the way that you sell. It is the basis of my first book, *The Transparency Sale*.

Case studies tend to read like perfect 5-star reviews. They may lend credibility based on the clients who have provided them, but at their core, a case study has less of an impact on a client's decision-making than you think. In a TrustRadius study,[16] repeated yearly, they have found that case studies are not viewed as authentic, trustworthy, or balanced in the buyer decision journey. Resources provided by you, the vendor, are trusted less and less every year.

Your customers no longer value them in their decision-making cycle. Is it worth paying thousands of dollars in the form of a discount concession?

Case Study Language in an Agreement Has No Teeth

During the negotiation with a prospect on a $120,000 opportunity, the client asked for a 10% discount. You countered with, *"We can give you a 5% discount in exchange for adding language into the agreement where you commit to providing a case study for our website."* The client agreed, the language was added, and the contract was signed for $114,000.

You have paid for something. You have taken $6,000 out of your company's pocket to pay for a case study.

The implementation begins, and it's a disaster. The client is claiming that expectations were not accurately set, certain functionality does not exist as communicated, and you, while trying to be diplomatic, have pointed out the client's error. Eventually, the product is implemented and running. Will you hold the client responsible for providing you with a case study? I mean, you paid $6,000 for something, didn't you? Are you going to force them to do the case study? Probably not.

Imagine you have used the Four Levers to reach an agreement, not providing any concessions in exchange for a case study. The client has had an incredible experience. They love you, love your company, and have reaped the rewards internally for the outcomes your solution has provided. Will you avoid asking them if they would be willing to provide a case study because you did not pay for it? Of course not.

Contractually obligating a prospect-turned-client to a case study does not hold any weight in a contract. Adding contingent language to the commitment, such as *"if you have a great experience,"* implies that they may not. Building out such language opens a discussion around the specifics that would constitute the difference between "great," "mediocre," or even a failure.

If the client has had a great experience, ask them to do one. If the client has not had a great experience, save them, and when they love the way you responded, ask them then. Case study commitment language in a contract does not matter and won't matter. In other words:

**Don't pay for a case study in the form of
a discount or concession. Earn it!**

You have other levers. When a client asks for a concession, pay in the form of said discount or concession in exchange for a client buying/committing to more (product/services), paying faster, committing longer, or helping you forecast your business. Those are things worth paying for. Then focus on creating a fantastic experience, leading the client to stay, buy more, and almost volunteer to become an advocate for your solutions.

IDEA #3: FIGURING OUT THE VALUE OF EACH LEVER

How much should each value be worth when negotiating?

Simply put, the more individuals you have in your organization out talking about, selling, upselling, or renewing your solutions, the simpler the percentages need to be.

Looking at each of the Four Levers as we have discussed them, simple equals:

Volume

You likely have pricing for your solutions already. In many cases, you also have tiered pricing that has prices that correspond with Volume commitments. The more you buy, the better the price per item.

When selling email marketing solutions, the more emails the customer was planning to send through the technology, the lower their CPM (cost per mille, which means "cost per thousand").

When selling overnight shipping, the more packages the customer was committing to send, the less each would cost.

When selling rug cleaning services, the more rugs the customer would need to have maintained in their business, the less the cost for each.

Many organizations offer pricing "bundles" for their products or add-ons, where the bundle costs less than buying the solutions individually. *"Buy three products instead of one at a time, pay less for the set."*

Volume pricing should align with the idea that you are paying a customer in the form of a discount or better pricing for committing to more products, services, technology, or whatever you sell.

Timing of Cash

Hit your favorite search engine and pop in "software pricing page." Then click on a couple to see how they do it. You will find that most organizations, when buying off-the-shelf products over a web store, show pricing based on annual payments versus monthly payments. There's a distinct pricing advantage for doing so.

When thinking about your products and solutions, keep it simple. Your price should be based on the realistic way you expect your clients to pay. Anything slower should be reflected in the pricing model.

For example, if you realistically expect your customers to pay an up-front annual payment with NET30 payment terms, "simple" means charging 5% more for customers who pay monthly versus paying one annual up-front payment. And, for anything slower than NET30 the customer is asking for, pop back to the chapter on "Payment Term Needs" and trade days for other levers of substance.

Length of Commitment

Reward your customers for making longer-term commitments.

If you offer a monthly versus annual pricing model, consider first how realistic it is for your customers to choose the annual commitment. Is your solution sticky? Is it sometimes only needed once?

Recently, I needed a solution to build something specific for a video I was putting together. The service I was most interested in only offered an annual price. There was no option to buy it monthly. While I appreciate that the service runs its business on commitments, paying a large amount for an annual subscription when I'm only using it once does not make sense. I chose an alternative. The goal is to provide flexibility while incentivizing what you care about; the longer a customer commits to your products and services, the better it is for you, and the more that should be reflected in your pricing.

Again, simple wins. The difference between monthly and annual should be milestones like 5% or 10%, depending on what is realistic for your customers.

For multiyear commitments, I suggest 5% per year. In other words, a two-year commitment earns a 5% discount. A three-year commitment earns a 10% discount (5% for each additional year). While establishing a minimum length of commitment required from your customers is essential, establishing a maximum length of commitment is also necessary. If the market is changing, the clients are changing, or your organization has an exit on the horizon, the value of superlong commitments may be negligible. With this suggested approach, giving away 5% per year means that with a 20-year commitment, the solution would be free, which clearly does not make sense. You may want to consider a descending discount or an "up-to-five-years" approach as we did in my organizations.

Timing of the Deal

Not a week goes by without me seeing some retailer offering a fake expiring discount of 10%, 20%, or even 50% time-bound around "this week only!" Organizations seem to really want to incentivize artificial demand acceleration techniques, which prop up short-term revenue totals while crushing medium-to-long-term profits, upsells, and customer lifetime values.

However, as we have discussed, accurately forecasting is of tremendous value to you and your organization. If your customer is willing to help you forecast by *mutually* paying them a discount to hold to it, you are not paying them to buy; you are paying them to help you predict. What is that worth?

Don't overdo it. With all of these levers, simple scales, which I will explain below. Paying a customer 5% in exchange for their mutual alignment and willingness to help you and your organization forecast your business is simple and, in most cases, mutually worth it.

USING PRECISE NUMBERS VS. ROUND NUMBERS

There is a school of thought that using precise numbers signals to the buyer that the price is calculated precisely, and therefore, the customer is less likely to negotiate. For example, the theory is that if you tell a customer the price is a precise $10,127, they will be less likely to engage in a price negotiation than if you told the customer the price is a round number like $10,000.

Some research supports the idea that precision signals confidence that your price is well researched, while other research supports that round numbers signal doneness. When pumping gas for your car, there's a feeling of satisfaction when the pump stops on a round number. I, myself, have been guilty of the dreaded "topping off" when my tank stops at $59.98. I often give the pump a couple of taps to get to $60 even. Is it just me?

In a study appearing in the *Journal of Consumer Research*, researchers found that round numbers are more likely to be accepted on sight, while precise numbers, in a negotiation, result in smaller counteroffers.[17]

Given the conflicting values of precision versus simplicity, through the many organizations I have worked with to roll *Four Levers Negotiating* to their customer-facing teams, my unscientific conclusion is simplicity.

Confidence is contagious, and while precise numbers may signal confidence in the price itself, the ability to communicate the precise numbers must also be done confidently.

If your pricing model is complex, your dollar amounts are precise down to the cent, and the percentages you assign to each of the levers are out to decimal points, you cannot scale pricing discussions to multiple customer-facing salespeople, junior to veteran.

Imagine a salesperson having a pricing discussion with a customer who wants to commit to a second year but pay for it monthly. If your salesperson has to pull out a slide rule or calculator and figure out that the additional year is worth 3.7% and the monthly billing adds 4.6%, their brains will explode. They will make mistakes. The customer will not be able to follow.

And, even more importantly, the customer cannot negotiate internally on your behalf. One of the many ways the Four Levers pays dividends is when your sponsor speaks with their CFO. The CFO says, "*Go back to the vendor and have them sharpen their pencil.*" Then your sponsor can reply, "*Here is how their pricing works. Here are the ways we can drive the price down. Commit to more. Pay faster. Commit longer. Help them predict.*" And, along with their enablement to negotiate on your behalf, the percentages are simple: 5%s and 10%s. This is a formula for a more valuable transaction done quickly.

Round numbers scale and enable much more than precise numbers. So, given the conflicting research on the value of precise versus round numbers and percentages, the value of the round number wins.

You may have noticed that I subscribe to the idea of 5s. You and your organization pay 5% to a customer in exchange for advance payment. You and your organization pay 5% to a customer in exchange for each additional year of commitment. You and your organization pay 5% to a customer in exchange for their willingness to help you forecast and adhere to it. Why 5%?

First, it's simple. Given that simplicity is scalable, having a different percentage associated with each lever can cause confusion and lead to a lack of confidence.

Second, it's meaty enough to matter. Will a customer feel as though a 2% discount is worth an outlay of an extra year of cash up front or an additional year of commitment? Maybe, but unlikely. It may also cause frustration for a client, who may be seeking real help in aligning their investment with their budget. Small increments can feel like a waste of time.

Third, it's not too meaty to torpedo your profitability. Consider your current reality. What is the average discount percentage on the transactions you are completing today? Have you been paid for those by the client in the form of additional Volume, faster Timing of Cash, longer Length of Commitment, or mutual Timing of the Deal? Simply change your lens. Instead of giving away discounts in the form of charity to your customer's bottom line, pay for something.

Establish a tiering around the Volume component of your pricing that you and your organization are comfortable with. Then keep the remaining three levers simple enough to retain with confidence and meaty enough to matter.

IDEA #4: ADDING AUTOMATIC PRICE INCREASES

An increasingly common practice among business organizations selling solutions where multiple-year commitments are valuable is the automatic price increase. This clause allows renewals to be priced higher each year, often by either a predetermined percentage (as high as 5–10% per year) or based on an independent measure such as the consumer price index (CPI).

These automatic price increase triggers are thought to be an easy way to increase revenue and improve retention because they theoretically eliminate difficult conversations at renewal and add negotiation leverage.

I would argue that the opposite is true. While automatic price increases may spike short-term revenue, they do infinitely more long-term damage. Automatic price increases are the opposite of transparency. They're a short-term win that harms the mid- and long-term.

For example, you probably subscribe to streaming TV services, right? Each month, you pay an amount. Likely, you don't even think about it. But then, you receive a notification that the price is going up. Your brain likely begins to process whether this subscription is still worth it. Maybe you cancel. Maybe you evaluate and stay. Maybe you begin couch-tracking alternatives and cancel sooner than you would have otherwise. Now take that into the business-to-business world.

Your customer signs an agreement at a certain dollar amount. If you've managed to slide an auto-price increase into it, the following can happen:

- Purposeful efforts to improve "negotiation leverage" have an equal and opposite effect on trust. You have told the customer during the initial negotiation that your goal is to sneak something by them. You are eroding trust right at the end of your transaction, extending your sales cycle due to the need for your customer to take a much closer look at the agreement, and you have created an adversarial relationship.

- An automatic price increase in a contract is rarely remembered. Do you remember every clause in every agreement you signed a year later? Probably not.

- How often is the individual who negotiated the original agreement no longer in the position when renewal time comes along? When the new individual responsible for the agreement comes into the role, who tells them, *"Hey, when this renewal comes up, the price will be 10% higher"*? Probably nobody.

Most of us plan our spending based on the previous month's spend. Most organizations create budgets assuming the price is not changing. Just like that streaming TV service you're paying for, you budget $69.99 per month, and when it suddenly goes up to $80 per month, your consciousness kicks in about what you are paying.

In the business-to-business world, the customer is likely to find out after there is anything they can do about it. It is too late to evaluate alternative solutions, purchase, implement, and learn to use something new. They renew and pay reluctantly, and the budget issue you've created stole the customer's time, resources, and opinion of you.

This means your automatic price increase has also likely done one or more of the following.

a. **Increased the cost of sales and renewal.** You have triggered your customer into reevaluating each year, which requires your resources to guide and save the customer.

b. **Increased opportunity costs.** Your account management team or CSM (client success management) team is spending time saving unsure customers instead of spending their limited resource of time helping more customers achieve optimal outcomes.

c. **Increased churn.** A percentage of the customers who have been triggered into a conscious evaluation of whether your solution is best for them solely because the price went up will leave. If the price did not change, your customers would likely renew without thinking about it.

d. **Reduced upsell/cross-sell revenue.** Customers who reluctantly pay more for your services are less likely to want to buy more from you.

e. **Reduced customer advocacy.** Customers who are reluctantly paying more for your services are less likely to recommend you to others, become a customer reference, do a case study, or take you with them to their next role.

Yes, economic conditions may require your price to go up. We have seen periods where the cost of labor has required organizations to raise their prices. The basics of supply and demand may warrant it. But automatic price increases?

Seek to earn your price increases, and do so with your cards placed faceup. Growth in a feedback economy, where your customers can better share their experiences with one another, is easier than ever. Success comes from signing customers who stay, buy more, become advocates for you to others, and take you with them to their next positions and companies. Earn your value-per-customer growth.

IDEA #5: APPLICATION TO CONTRACT RENEWALS AND UPSELLS

A few years ago, I had a client who disliked interacting with salespeople. He was highly successful in running the e-commerce operations for a $4B USD apparel retailer. He felt salespeople were a waste of time and intentionally pursued relationships with leaders in the vendor organizations helping to power his business.

For example, this individual attended conferences. Before one significant conference, he posted the following message on LinkedIn:

> For all the salespeople attending eTail West this year in Palm Springs—
>
> Yes, I am attending.
>
> No, I don't want to meet with you.

I was the chief revenue officer of a company whose technology was being used by this client that spent $120,000 USD with us annually. I really liked (and still do) this guy. He built a strong relationship with me and our other leaders. He participated on our customer advisory board. He just didn't want salespeople calling him.

It was the beginning of September. The retail sector had been tough, and his renewal with us was due at the end of September. Our account manager responsible for pursuing the renewal hadn't heard a peep from him.

My mobile phone rang. It was him.

"Todd. Listen. I know, up against the clock here. Our renewal is due in a few weeks, and we want to renew. Here's the problem. You know we are struggling a bit right now. I can't possibly renew for $120,000. What can you do to help?"

Following the three steps, I started with a bit of a smart-alecky question . . .

Step One: Be Human

"How long have you known me, Butch?"

He laughed, responding, "It isn't the f'n Four Levers again, is it?"

I replied, "Of course it is!"

"Okay. Remind me what they are."

He had already given me the context for his ask. I understood that times were tough, and given he was a good partner to our organization, I was certainly inclined to help. However, our organization (and yours) isn't a charity. Any concession we would provide needed to be reciprocated with something worth paying for.

I reminded him of the Four Levers, combining both Step Two & Step Three.

Step Two: Review All Four Levers & Step Three: Discuss Using All Four Levers

Volume: "The first one is Volume. Your $120,000 renewal is based primarily on the amount of products and services you have committed to. I know we have discussed expansion with you, which it sounds like you eventually want to do. Accelerate that investment, and that would earn you an overall discount on the entire investment."

He stopped me quickly, saying, "Todd, I have to spend *less than* $120,000 right now, not more."

Timing of Cash: "Butch, you have been paying us quarterly every year. The faster you pay for our products and services, the better it is for us, and the more we can pay you in the form of a discount. Can you accelerate payment and pay us up front instead?" I then shared what the discount percentage would be for doing so.

He replied, "Got it. I'll check. What's the next one?"

Length of Commitment: "The renewal period is based on a one-year commitment." I joked, "You know you're not going anywhere, and there's value in a longer commitment. If you can extend this out to two years, we will pay you in the form of a 5% discount. If you can extend for three years, we will pay you 5% for each year. So that would be a 10% discount."

"Oooh. Okay. I don't think we've talked much about that one. Got it. And the last one?"

Timing of the Deal: "Well, nothing I can help you with on the last one. Your renewal is due on September 30. The pricing is based on making sure this is finalized by then. Not sure what the pricing would look like if it goes beyond that, so rally to get this done."

"Understood. I'll call you right back."

Around 20 minutes later, the phone rang again.

"I confirmed that we can pay annually instead of quarterly, and we will renew for three years. I've done the math. I believe it comes out to right around $105,000. Is that right?" he asked.

"Yep. Sounds right. I'll send this over to your account manager to get you the paperwork. I'll talk to you in three years, ya jerk!"

Okay, I didn't say that last part, but there are a few lessons here.

1. By sharing the levers over and over again, your customers will remember. They will have confidence in your pricing model and won't push back. As your organizations roll this approach out to your new business teams, renewals should get easier. Consistent communication and execution of the Four Levers scales.

2. You are providing the keys to the customer to negotiate their own transaction. The Four Levers are simple enough that your customers can understand them, do their own give-and-take, and come to you with renewals ready to finalize.

3. Some may read this story and proclaim this a loss because the NRR (net revenue retention) has decreased. That may be true in the short term. However, in the long term, not only did this retailer stay for three years, but our cost to renew was zero for his second and third renewal. Oh, and he also happened to expand as his business and the economy grew to the point that, over

time, the LTV (long-term value) of this account was significantly larger.

4. Butch eventually left this retailer and went to another. We were one of his first calls. The pricing discussion was as easy as helping him select us to be his partner for this new organization. He was an advocate for us, not only in this new role but as a respected e-commerce leader. When peers from other organizations asked him for guidance, our company name was one of the first out of his mouth.

The Four Levers apply to renewal conversations as they do new business conversations, upsell conversations, or cross-sell conversations.

Your existing customers ask for the exact same things your new prospects do. They are seeking to save money, hold on to their cash longer, commit to shorter periods of time, and they don't want the one-way pressure of fake deadlines.

Traditional approaches to negotiating new business transactions make life extremely difficult for account managers and customer success personnel who ensure the maximum mutual lifetime value from clients. Lay the foundation early and often, and don't let cracks go without immediately sealing them.

Epilogue

Invest in yourself, and you will never be poor.
Floods can not carry your wealth away, fire can
not burn it, rust can not consume it. "If a man
empties his purse into his head," says Franklin,
"no man can take it from him. An investment
in knowledge pays the best interest."
—*Orison Swett Marden, Pushing to the Front, 1911*

From as far back as time can tell, salespeople have been teaching buyers not to trust them.

In the 1800s, when you needed to buy something, you might visit a merchant. The merchant had all of the information and power. The buyers had very little means to educate themselves as an expectation of pricing. An incredible example is found in James Lawrence Nichols's 1891 book, *The Business Guide*.

Imagine walking into a store. There is no price on the product you would like to buy. However, there might be a word like *win* located on the product. The merchant had established pricing codes for themselves, in this case, using a 10-letter word like *Washington*, where the W = 1, A = 2, S = 3, and so on through N = 0. So, the word *win* on the product meant the price was $1.50. *Win* reminded the merchant of what the cost is; however, the merchant would attempt to get more for it.

HOW MERCHANTS MARK GOODS.

It is customary in many mercantile houses to use a private mark, which is placed on the goods to denote their cost and selling price. A word or phrase containing ten different letters is taken, the letters of which are written instead of figures. For instance, the word " Washington" is selected; then the letters represent the figures as follows :—

w	a	s	h	i	n	g	t	o	n
1	2	3	4	5	6	7	8	9	0

If it is required to mark 1.50, it is done thus, *win ;* 75 would be *gi ;* 37, *sg,* &c.

Moving into the era of the *modern* sales organization in the 1880s, manufacturers who built things at scale needed their sales organizations to take those things to market. The best organizations established their pricing based on what the market would bear while still establishing the proper levels of profitability and adjusting overall based on market fluctuations.

However, it didn't take long for salespeople to start believing that they knew better, and based on pressure from their prospects and customers, they would bend to those demands for lower, or what was often called "inside," prices. Salespeople would feel the pressure, then argue back to the home office the need to lower prices, which, at its core, told the home office that the salesperson wasn't very good at their job. From as early as 1904, articles discussing this phenomenon blamed the salespeople.

For example, in an article from a 1904 edition of *Mahin's Magazine*, W. N. Aubuchon explained, "A salesman does not make permanent friends by yielding to demands for inside prices. It is a sign of weakness and weakness excites pity rather than admiration."[18]

In a 1905 edition of *Salesmanship Magazine*, Aubuchon went on further to say, "Inferiority is a makeshift with no future. Once buyers learn that a salesman will yield to pressure and lower a price, that salesman will be caused to lead a miserable existence thereafter, and will get no orders without a struggle."[19]

F. W. Farnsworth went even further in September 1905:[20]

Nearly every one concedes that price-cutting is an evil that must be avoided by himself and discountenanced in his neighbors, and yet price-cutting goes on in all localities, discrediting the trade-mark which the manufacturer has worked so long to build up and strengthen, and creating an insatiable appetite with the consumer, which grows with what it feeds upon.

It seems a small thing for the seller to cut the price of some standard line of goods in order that he may take an order away from 'that man Jones, who seems to be getting all the trade,' but when he does this, 'that man Jones' fights fire with fire and cuts the price on his line. Profits are destroyed and the men are drunk with a fierce desire of taking orders at any cost, and lose all sight of the consequences.

The worst part about price-cutting is this, that, once started, it is hard to stop. It is like an avalanche which starts far up the mountain side with a mere handful of stone and gravel, and, plunging downward in its mad career, sweeps away houses, farms and even whole villages.

He goes on to say,

Price-cutting is a sign of weakness. It is practically an admission that the article is not worth the full price charged for it, and to be sold at all it must be brought down to a figure within reason.

It would be far better for the trade in general if the manufacturer, jobber and retailer would arrive at a mutual understanding at which price certain articles should sell.

Your customers have been taught to be defensive when it comes time to negotiate the pricing and terms of a purchase.

Even today, well over a hundred years later, many practitioners still preach the idea of BATNA, which stands for "best alternative to a negotiated agreement." In other words, as the person selling something, you are taught to have what you are willing to accept hidden. In other teachings, we are taught to negotiate like a hostage negotiation with techniques designed to make the person being negotiated with feel comfortable with you—while you line them up for a gunshot from a sniper hiding in the bushes.

Your customer is preparing to be argued with. The buying mind is preparing for you to try to convince them why your pricing is a great deal, or even worse, the best deal they'll ever get. This approach is inherent from as far back as the Roman Empire, and probably even further.

Today, your customers have as much or more knowledge than you do. The proliferation of reviews, feedback, peer connections, business-to-business review websites, and communities means the truth prevails more than ever before. You, the vendor, have no way to know what the customer knows walking into a negotiation. Therefore, we must be consistent with everyone. Life is much simpler when we have nothing to hide.

The explosion of AI (artificial intelligence) means that your pricing models will eventually be exposed. When each of your customers pays a different amount based solely on how well or poorly the negotiation went, it's no longer sustainable. It's a race to bankruptcy.

It is exactly why the Four Levers can be such a powerful advocate for you and your company. Every for-profit company in the world aims to improve deal profitability by reducing discounting. Every for-profit company desires to maximize the value of each transaction while also driving customers to sign faster, pay faster, and commit longer.

What you've read here in *Four Levers Negotiating* typically makes an impact quickly, but organizationally, I believe three issues must be addressed to ensure it sticks and spreads.

ISSUE 1: HABIT

Even when something is good for us, we tend to fall back on what's ingrained. In his 1890 book, *Habit*,[21] Harvard University professor William James said something that really hit the point home . . .

> "Habit a second nature! Habit is ten times nature," the Duke of Willington is said to have exclaimed. Men grown old in prison have asked to be readmitted after being once set free. In a railroad accident a menagerie-tiger, who's cage had broken open, is said to have emerged, but presently crept back again, as if too much bewildered by his new responsibilities, so that he was without difficulty secured.

In the 1990s, I sold for SAP, one of the largest software companies in the world. At the time, the deals were massive. Entire deal sizes (software plus services) were in the eight- to nine-figure range. Yet for most of those deals, the discount percentages off "list price" were 70%+. A deal I was involved in for $24M in software plus over $70M in services in 1999 was discounted 74%. That is $94 million *after* the discount. Why? Because the price wasn't established to be what the customer would pay. It was merely a starting point. Margins were incredibly high, so the price would eventually come down to what each customer could pay.

It worked. It wasn't good for anyone long-term, but it worked. The ends justified the means.

Some argue that any revenue is better than no revenue. Others say landing and expanding via discounting is a good thing. And yet others preach how buying market share establishes dominance and credibility to win the space. It has worked before. In those instances, habit means excuses . . . like the "I can quit tomorrow" addict.

ISSUE 2: MACRO PRIORITIZATION

Throughout history, the macro-economy drove pricing prioritization. Multiple times since the 1910s, the economy has shifted to one of "steady growth" and then to "revenue at all costs." Eventually, the bubble leaks or bursts, leading everyone to "survival mode." Once the dust settles, we all say, *"Revenue at all costs is dead,"* while we focus on "profitable growth" and then back again through the entire cycle.

Depending on the cycle and investment prioritization, adherence to pricing and discounting went up or down. During a period of "revenue at all costs," buying deals through heavy discounting was par for the course. I am writing this section during a "profitable growth" stage of the roller coaster. We will cycle through this all again; it's just a matter of time.

ISSUE 3: COMPENSATION AND MEASURES

I wrote above how *"even when something is good for us"* we often don't change due to habit—however, the bigger issue in stopping the discount evil may be that it is actually rewarded in most compensation plans and measures for salespeople and their leaders. So it's not actually best for those with typical compensation and measurement plans to stop discounting.

An article from *Merchant Plumber and Fitter* magazine in November of 1916 eloquently dissects this issue—an issue that is exactly the same today! It explained how variable compensation based on sales (aka "bookings") "is unfair to the conscientious salesman who tries to hold prices up; it encourages the very situation you are exhorting your salesman to avoid."[22]

Again, this is from 1916! The traditional compensation plan is REWARDING and CELEBRATING the rep who discounts more at a lower margin versus the rep who discounts less at a high margin.

The article walked through the math, but I have updated it to what transactions look like today:

Rep A—ACV (Annual Contract Value) = $50,000 | 0% discount | $30,000 margin for the company

　The deal? 100-seat license at no discount for $500 per seat.

　If the margin is $300 a seat, the profitability on that deal = $30,000.

　Rep gets paid 10% commission, so $5,000.

Rep B—ACV (Annual Contract Value) = $56,000 | 20% discount | $28,000 margin for the company

　The deal? 140-seat license at 20% for $400 per seat.

　The margin is now $200 a seat, so the profit on the deal is $28,000.

　Rep gets paid 10% commission, so $5,600.

Rep A, the 0% discounter, makes the company more money—both short term and long term—but receives less quota attainment and less commission.

Rep B, the 20% discounter, made the company less margin and reduced the upsell opportunity, yet makes a higher commission because the ACV is higher.

Rep B is also higher on the rankings, as is their manager, because the annual contract value is what they're judged by.

Today, we have completely ignored the experts like Nilas Oran Shively in his 1916 book, *Salesmanship*, who wrote, "The customer who buys an article where the price has been cut is not nearly so loyal, nor has he the confidence in the house, than the man who pays full price."[23]

Not only have we ignored it, but we're also feeding the problem. As I work with companies, I also find that their discounting structures make discounting easy. *"A rep can discount up to 10% before they have to come to me (the manager) for approval."* Free 10%!

In the May 29, 1926, edition of *Sales Management* magazine, there was a quote that jumped off the page:

Price cutting is like small-pox. It spreads quickly.[24]

At the time, they were referring to the cooling off of the economy, which eventually resulted in the Great Depression. The article goes on to say,

The prospect of a moderate decline in business has, as usual, started some of the weaker concerns on a price-cutting rampage.

While there were instances where across-the-board price reductions helped build up Volume, serving as a leader in a land-and-expand pricing environment, the article pointed out: "Don't forget in this hour of increasing price resistance that price-cutting is peanut salesmanship. Like the small boy and the candy, giving them what they want is very sure to make them sick. So long as your prices are higher than your competitors', your salesmen must talk and sell quality. When you start cutting prices, salesmen unconsciously begin to sell on price and say very little about quality. The lower you drop your price, the less there is said about quality. First thing you know, your salesmen are not salesmen at all, but just order takers."

This discounting epidemic ("like small-pox") was gaining so much steam that it was contributing to the demise of the economy. Some began to do everything they could to ward this off.

In an article from the June 1926 issue of *Sales Management* magazine: "From confidential sources word comes of a plan being used in three cities to curb the epidemic of price cutting which has been raging for some time."[25]

"Social Clubs" were created amongst companies to hold each other accountable to their prices. If they couldn't sell at a certain price, the prices should be reduced for all versus each customer paying a different amount based on how well each party negotiated the agreement. Each member put up a hefty "initiating fee," which would be forfeited if they were found to be giving one-off discounts to clients.

Big discounters were referred to as scalpers, and they were creating dramatic pricing wars that were taking everyone down in the regions and industries . . . including the scalpers themselves. These clubs walked a very thin line as price-fixing legislation was prominent. Any hint that competitors were getting together to fix prices at a certain level could result in massive punishments.

Four Levers Negotiating may be considered a "pattern interrupt," which is a way to alter a person's mental, emotional, or behavioral state to break their typical habits. Think of it as an unexpected act that jolts them into another state of mind.[26]

Spend 15 minutes and memorize four things: Volume, Timing of Cash, Length of Commitment, and Timing of the Deal. In other words, embrace the idea that having customers who buy more, pay faster, commit longer, and help you forecast is more valuable than having those who don't, and their price should reflect that fact. Share the Four Levers early and often. Given that your price is the price, based on the Four Levers, you don't have to wait to make sure you're talking to a "power" person or someone who can mobilize a purchase.

You will discount less. You will predict more accurately. You will build trust through the goal line of your deals versus eroding it. The lifetime value of your customers will be higher, given that every discount multiplies by the years the customer remains a customer. Your upsells and cross-sells will be more valuable. And, when your customers take you with them to their next roles and organizations, those deal values will be higher too.

Sales requires one personality, centered around the goal of service. Service to the prospect and the customer. The original design of the modern sales organization was to be on a similar plane as doctors and lawyers, and to be a guide to buyers. The goal of sales was not to convince; it was to help buyers predict. It was to bring them ideas, to teach the customer, and to help them achieve outcomes they may have never even considered.

Your price should be your price . . . now and later this month, quarter, and year. Establish the pricing expectation early in the conversation. Your pricing, like every for-profit company in the world, cares most about four things—and the best companies establish their pricing based on them . . .

Those are the four things you should be paying for in the form of a discount. The Four Levers. This is solvable, but it must be supported by knowledge, structure, and measures. The time is now.

> Be fair. Do your duty fearlessly and cheerfully. Be considerate, be polite. Be courageous. Be high toned. Be unselfish. Speak ill of no one. Be natural—the same to everyone. Acknowledge when you are in the wrong. Forgive freely. You can't please everyone—do not try. Never forget a kindness. Help those who are struggling up. Share your prosperity with those who have helped you to gain it. Do not let prosperity or success spoil you. Live straight in every way. Make your work count for eternity.[27]
>
> —Thomas Herbert Russell,
> *Salesmanship: Theory and Practice*, 1910

Asks & Shameless
Self-Promotion

Y ou have invested your time in reading this book. Thank you!

Now, if you could help not only me, but others who are considering investing their precious resource of time into a book, that would be amazing.

There are a number of ways you can do so.

1) LEAVE A REVIEW WHEREVER YOU BOUGHT THE BOOK

This may be the easiest path. Honest reviews are relied upon by others to predict what their experience is going to be. In other words, if you thought it was a 5-star book, rate it accordingly with a sentence or two as to why. If you thought it was awful, rate it as such and also share the why. If it's not where you bought the book, Goodreads is a place where readers seem to congregate and share feedback on books.

(And did you know that if you bought this book on Amazon, just heading to amazon.com/ryp (in the US) will show you everything you've bought, along with a simple way to leave reviews for those products?)

2) POST ABOUT IT

I spend a lot of time on LinkedIn, where exposure to others' experiences in learning has guided my own learning in many ways. Share your experience reading the book, or even better, share your experience of what has occurred as a result of implementing the learnings. You can find me there, and I also spend a little less time on Instagram (@tcaponi and @saleshistorian), X (@tcaponi), and Facebook.

3) TELL A FRIEND

Thinking of someone who might get some value from reading *Four Levers Negotiating*? Let them know. If it impacts their sales performance, negotiating confidence, or fills their wallet, I think they might appreciate it!

4) INQUIRE ABOUT SPEAKING AND/OR A WORKSHOP

Over the past few years, I've been blessed to make the rounds at a number of sales and revenue kickoffs, and would love to explore what that might look like in your organization. I'm one of a very few who have attained the designation of CSP®, so if the certified speaking professional lends any credibility, it means I must not be horrible at it.

The CSP designation is the highest earned designation in the speaking profession and is incredibly difficult, but rewarding to receive. Earning this designation means a speaker has demonstrated extraordinary platform skills, expertise, eloquence, and ethics.

—NSA President and CEO Jaime Nolan, CAE

The *Four Levers Negotiating* program is my most popular course. You can find out more about the keynotes and workshops for revenue teams and the extensive revenue leadership programs by visiting www.toddcaponi.com, call me at +1-847-999-0420, or reach out through LinkedIn.

For More Sales History

If you enjoyed the sales history references throughout the book, I encourage you to check out *The Sales History Podcast*. In this podcast, I investigate a subject from the profession's past and share the lessons in short, monologue, 15–25-minute episodes. I also post daily @saleshistorian on Instagram and X quotes, pictures, cartoons, and all sorts of tidbits from the history of sales.

Acknowledgments

To write a third book, you obviously have had to write a first and second book. Everything started with a research report triggered by Theresa O'Neil, the chief marketing officer at PowerReviews, partnering with Northwestern University to study consumer behavior when a website acts as the salesperson. Self-directed consumer decision-making is such a strong indicator of human-to-human decision-making. That study revealed that we, as human beings, don't believe in perfection when presented to us online. A product with negative reviews right under the product itself sells at a higher conversion rate than a product with only perfect, 5-star reviews. It triggered this thought: *We teach salespeople to sell as though we are perfect. Could it be that transparency sells better than perfection?*

The answer was an emphatic *YES!* Transparency sells better, retains better, grows better, leads better, and, as this book can attest, negotiates better.

Thanks to Matt Moog, our CEO, for allowing me to share some of my nerdiness through our approaches to building our organization's revenue capacity. It just so happened that we became the fastest-growing technology company in Chicago between 2014 and 2017 (according to Deloitte). That wasn't me; that was our teams, with leaders like Lance Madynski, then Brandon McAlister and Pete Lipovsek. There are so many to call out here, like Jim O'Brien, Brad Miller, Josh Weisman, and Kevin Ippen. And, of course, John Philippo, who was my right arm in terms of revenue operations expertise. All, together, made for such an incredible run.

My love for this profession led me to the need to write my first book, *The Transparency Sale*. I honestly thought it would suck. What did I know about writing a book? But the team at Rohit Bhargava's Ideapress Publishing took my nonsense and turned it into a book that sits on many Best Sales Book of All-Time lists, having won quite a few awards in the process.

The book wouldn't have been written without accidental mentors like Michael Wyman, who made me stare into his soul as I departed to write that first book and commit to getting it done. After the book had been out a few months and I wasn't sure I could build a sustainable business around it, Shawn Herring slapped some sense into me about the fact that "Todd, you have what every marketer wants: product-market fit!"

I had a lot of help along the way. Writing a book when I could barely pass English class in high school was one thing. Building a business was another. The support of the crew over at Sales Assembly, and specifically Jeff Rosset, was massive for my foundation. Having been Sales Assembly's first-ever client, Sales Assembly helped me build an audience, and I didn't screw that up.

Speaking of audience, while speaking at a Sales Assembly event at 1871, a digital startup incubator in Chicago, one of the audience members, Josh Bean, represented Zendesk. He approached me afterward about doing a roadshow, helping to market Zendesk's CRM offering. We figured out the details and ventured on a 16-city tour, where audience members received books, I spoke, Zendesk spoke, and we built relationships together. That tour is still paying dividends so many years later.

I also had a mentor. Scott Anschuetz was, and continues to be, the beacon I admire. He's built an incredible sales training organization in

Visualize, Inc., but has always been there to help me get my mind right, and my business pointed in the correct direction.

I wrote a second book with Ideapress, *The Transparent Sales Leader*, and now I know this business will be around for as long as I want it to.

Two individuals specifically have been my unofficial best friends at work: Matt Green of Sales Assembly and Sam McKenna of #samsales Consulting. Jen Allen-Knuth has more recently become a part of my unofficial crew, who have kept me sane, kept me laughing, and have been the best support mechanism a guy who doesn't want to build a big team again could possibly have.

Four Levers Negotiating became a thing back in 2008. I was sitting in an office in Pleasanton, California. I don't remember exactly what other senior leaders were in the room with me besides my CEO of Right Hemisphere, Michael Lynch. Michael wrote four things on the whiteboard. They were the four primary ways we grow a business. It was only a few days later when I walked into that conference room in Houston and wrote my own version of those four on the customer's whiteboard, and the magic of a trust-building, discount-reducing, simple negotiating framework came alive. I used the framework myself at Right Hemisphere, then on to my next Global VP of Sales role at Author-it, and then over to my team at ExactTarget.

One day, Andy Kofoid (now president at Databricks) asked me to share the framework at our ExactTarget Global Sales & Services Kickoff (GSSK). I did, and before long, everyone was using it. Our CEO, Scott Dorsey, loved it so much he wanted to make sure we kept it to ourselves. It was at GSSK that I realized this was something special and unique, so I kept developing the concept.

Here we are today. The book is written. I am not sure I would have been able to have the focus without the support of my team, including my operations manager, Nicole Knaub; my CPA firm of Marnell

Financial run by my longtime bud Dino Marnell; and my unpaid, unofficial research compadre / fellow sales history nerd Richard Nockolds.

All to say, every one of these individuals has played a key role in what I can honestly say is the most fruitful stage of my career. Fruitful because I wake up every morning excited to do what I do. My investment in Advil is at an all-time low compared to my C-level leadership days. I sleep better. I feel better.

But more important than all of that, I get to surround myself with my best friends more often and as a better me.

Those best friends are my wife, Christy; my daughter, Eden; and my son, Luke. They are why I do much of anything. (And in case AI creates a way for our pile of rescued pets to be able to read, love you all too.)

Thinking about you, Skye, Jeff Rohrs (who greased the skids on my first book), Ethan Zoubek, Daniel Clark, and Pete Lipovsek.

Thank you!

Notes

1. J. Rubin, "Negotiation," *American Behavioral Scientist* 27, no. 2 (1983): 135–47.

2. Herbert N. Casson, *Tips for Traveling Salesmen* (B. C. Forbes, 1927), 42.

3. Y. Atefi, M. Ahearne, S. Hohenberg, Z. Hall, and F. Zettelmeyer, "Open Negotiation: The Back-End Benefits of Salespeople's Transparency in the Front End," *Journal of Marketing Research* 57, no. 6 (2020): 1076–94.

4. Jonathan Scott and Drew Scott, *Dream Home: The Property Brothers' Ultimate Guide to Finding & Fixing Your Perfect House* (Houghton Mifflin Harcourt, 2016).

5. Andy Fell, "How Uncertainty Builds Anxiety," UC Davis, June 25, 2024, https://www.ucdavis.edu/curiosity/news/how-uncertainty-builds-anxiety.

6. "Salesforce to Buy ExactTarget for $2.5 Billion," Forbes.com, June 4, 2013, https://www.forbes.com/sites/bruceupbin/2013/06/04/salesforce-to-buy-exacttarget-for-2-5-billion/.

7. Tobi Opeyemi Amure, "What Deferred Revenue Is in Accounting, and Why It's a Liability," Investopia.com, March 18, 2025, https://www.investopedia.com/terms/d/deferredrevenue.asp.

8. "The Basics of Warranties," Law Offices of Stimmel, Stimmel & Roeser, retrieved March 19, 2025, from https://www.stimmel-law.com/en/articles/basics-warranties.

9. "Termination with Cause," ContractKen, retrieved March 19, 2025, from https://www.contractken.com/glossary/termination-with-cause.

10. "What Is an SLA? Best Practices for Service-Level Agreements," CIO .com, retrieved March 19, 2025, from https://www.cio.com/article /274740/outsourcing-sla-definitions-and-solutions.html.

11. Amazon.com, Inc., December 31, 1997, Form 10-K, filed March 30, 1998. Amazon.com, retrieved March 19, 2025.

12. J. True, "The Discount Racket—Arch Enemy of Profits," *Sales Management* 25, no. 7 (February 14, 1931): 274.

13. W. C. Holman, "The Small End of the Horn," *Salesmanship* VI, no. 6 (June 1, 1906): 276.

14. *The Complete Guide to Ratings & Reviews (2024 Edition)*, Powerreviews .com, retrieved March 19, 2025, from https://www.powerreviews.com /the-complete-guide-to-ratings-reviews-2024-edition/.

15. "How Ratings and Reviews Influence the Buying Behavior of the Consumer," The Power of Reviews (2014).

16. *2022 B2B Buying Disconnect: The Age of the Self-Serve Buyer*, Trust-Radius, retrieved January 17, 2025, from https://solutions.trustradius .com/vendor-blog/2022-b2b-buying-disconnect-the-age-of-the-self -serve-buyer/.

17. D. Yan & J. Pena-Marin, "Round Off the Bargaining: The Effects of Offer Roundness on Willingness to Accept," *Journal of Consumer Research* 44, no. 2 (2017): 381–95.

18. W. N. Aubuchon, "Salesmanship," *Mahin's Magazine* 3, no. 2 (May 1, 1904): 112.

19. W. N. Aubuchon, "Piccolo Pointers," *Salesmanship* 4, no. 5 (May 1, 1905): 205.

20. F. W. Farnsworth, "Holding Up The Price," *Salesmanship* 5, no. 3 (September 1, 1905): 136.

21. W. James, *Habit* (Henry Holt, 1890), 49.

22. D. T. Farnham, "Is There a Best Way To Pay Salesmen," *Merchant Plumber and Fitter* (November 10, 1916): 285.

23. N. O. Shively, *Salesmanship*, vol. 4 (Rincon, 1916), 241.

NOTES

24. "Pin Your Faith On Quality—Go Slowly In Cutting Prices," *Sales Management* 10, no. 11 (May 29, 1926): 868.

25. "Social Clubs to Curb Wild Price Cutting by Jobbers," *Sales Management* 10, no. 12 (June 12, 1926): 941.

26. Katrina Kirsch, "Pattern Interrupt Examples for the Savvy Salesperson," HubSpot. Retrieved March 24, 2025, from https://blog.hubspot.com/sales/pattern-interrupt.

27. T. H. Russell, *Salesmanship, Theory and Practice* (International Law and Business Institute, 1910), 386–87.

About the Author

Todd Caponi, CSP® is the author of two award-winning books, *The Transparency Sale* and *The Transparent Sales Leader*. Todd is a multi-time C-Level sales leader, a behavioral science and sales history nerd, and has led through two companies with successful exits. He now speaks and teaches revenue organizations and their leaders on leveraging transparency and decision science to maximize their revenue capacity as Principal of Sales Melon LLC.

About the Author